GOETHE

D·I·W·GÖTHE

GOETHE AS A YOUNG MAN
FROM THE ENGRAVING BY D. CHODOWIECKI
After the painting by G. M. Kraus (Weimar, 1776)

GOETHE

BY

BENEDETTO CROCE

WITH AN INTRODUCTION BY

DOUGLAS AINSLIE

AND A PORTRAIT

KENNIKAT PRESS

Port Washington, N. Y./London

GOETHE

First published in 1923
Reissued in 1970 by Kennikat Press
Library of Congress Catalog Card No: 78-103179
SBN 8046-0816-4

Manufactured by Taylor Publishing Company   Dallas, Texas

INTRODUCTION

BENEDETTO CROCE'S philosophy and criticism are, I believe, becoming known every year to wider circles, both on the North American continent and among ourselves. His philosophy was the first side of his genius which I was able to offer the English-speaking world, and the first to appear of the four volumes, now in its second English edition, was the *Æsthetic.* Readers of this treatise will find its principles underlying the whole of Croce's criticism ; alone among great philosophers he has proved his theories by applying them to life and literature.

The main thing to remember in reading his critical essays is that for Croce the æsthetic or artistic faculty is one of the eternal forms of the human spirit, distinct, but not separate, alike from the ethical and economic activities, which, with the logical, complete the entire circle of the human spirit. There is no fifth activity to be added to them, and all problems presented by any form of life are therefore to be resolved either into one of these or a combination of them. The æsthetic activity, which might also be loosely termed artistic creation, is not an exclusive appanage of poets and artists ; we all possess it to a greater or less degree ; otherwise it would be impossible for the public to enjoy or in any way understand poem or picture, music or statuary. The point, therefore, is that æsthetic capacity is, in philosophical language, *quantitative*, not qualitative, as has hitherto often been believed. There is no attribute of the creator in art differentiating him *altogether* from his fellow-men. He is simply a *richer* man, richer, that is to say, in those gifts which alone really count in life. The very great poets are supreme examples of endowment in æsthetic riches ; their intuitions are wider, deeper, and above all more frequent, than those of lesser men.

Was Goethe a very great poet ? Croce considers this to have certainly been so ; others, on the contrary, and among ourselves my friend Sir George Douglas, have taken up a rather less enthusiastic attitude to the presiding genius of Weimar, while, of course, admitting the great value of some of his production. Earlier writers in Great Britain, such as Carlyle, who published an English version of *Wilhelm Meisters Lehrjahre* in 1824 and followed it up with a couple of articles in the *Foreign Review*, afterwards reprinted, did much, on the other hand, to set Goethe upon a pinnacle. He was one of the " heroes," and therefore, for Carlyle, above that criticism which later and better equipped minds have been able to bring to bear upon the poetry and life of the author of *Faust*. Carlyle's immense prestige was, indeed, for many years responsible for the exaggerated admiration for Goethe's work as a whole, which has reigned in our country. Much of it, as Croce here points out with admirable clarity, is frankly bad or inferior, and if taken as representative, obscures our appreciation of his best work.

Yet who does not admire Goethe ? Those only who do not know him at his best. For Goethe is, of course, far more than a German ; he is one of the very few great European poets of the modern world.

My wish would have been to deal myself with the translation of Croce's illuminative work, as with those on Shakespeare, Dante,

Ariosto, and other poets; but my own work has come between, and to delay the essay on Goethe taking its place beside those other great ones, would have been to deprive thousands on both sides of the Atlantic of a new and sure guide to "pure pleasure," in the Greek sense.

Pleasure is a word often on one's lips in reading Goethe, the divine amateur, who was also a supreme artist in life.

Another charming characteristic of Goethe which should win to his side the most ardent francophils, is surely that intrepid detachment of his, a detachment which did not flinch even before the Napoleonic invasion of his country and led him to refuse to speak ill of the French, even when they were in occupation of Germany. Certainly, with Einstein and those illustrious few others among the German professors, he would have refused to sign the ill-famed manifesto of hatred for the Allies. Goethe, in fact, never lost his balance, and this detachment was not indifference, but always the nice adjustment of immense opposing forces, the domination of the material, i.e. life and art.

Goethe has especial interest for many Italians, as he drew so much of his inspiration from Italy, and in Benedetto Croce he has an admirer as firm as any of his out-and-out partisans, yet also a critic ; for Croce the student of Hegel is also the author of *What is Living and What is Dead* of Hegel, and never hesitates to point out where, with Goethe, inspiration fails or takes a false route—dies in fact as often it did—though it must also be admitted that he usually returned to the right route of his own accord. The wanderings of Goethe belong properly to biography, not to this volume; for, as Croce points out, he does not here treat in detail the many other sides of Goethe's personality, save in so far as they affect the consideration of his poetical work. Thus of the Italian sources of much of Goethe's inspiration, he merely says that no one else ever reaped such a harvest as he did, in that land of enchantment to poets of all nations. Of formal philosophy, too, he says little, beyond pointing out that Goethe does not there excel, but is rather full of wisdom, the wisdom of life, always at work with all his faculties, never separating feeling and thought or working upon externals, as is the pedant's way. On every page, I believe, the readers of this book will find coin of thought to repay them fifty-fold its price—of thought,

to my mind, deeper and greater than
Goethe's. "Enemies as steps in the development of complete self-conquest—one
should explore the explorable and calmly
worship the Inexplorable—there is nothing
exact in mathematics but their own exact-
ness—what poets really do rather than what
they fancy they do," and so on; such phrases
as these open vistas indeed, and when Croce
begins to deal with the works in detail, we
have the feeling of a very clear mirror held
up before a magnificent forest; where, amid
the boles of mighty oaks, there is much tangle
of picturesque underwood, not without, here
and there, an admixture of aconite, adders,
and stinging nettles, vast expanses of loose-
strife and verdant boggy danger. For Croce
does not scruple to put his finger at once
upon the weak or shady spots—as when he
says calmly of Faust: "Goethe's error here
lay in attempting to answer with a poetical
work the question as to the value of human life.

Despite his many adventures, Goethe was
able to preserve until the end that state
of robust wisdom, which got the better of
his taste for doubtful female company (where,
as Croce admits, he found some of his
most valuable material). He always upheld

the importance and superiority of marriage as an ethical spiritual force superior to any other tie between the sexes, and one of the most remarkable of Goethe's view-points seems to be that of the pure idea of morality as connected with the most lofty womanliness and becoming the " full affirmation of human liberty."

What may be called the by-products of Goethe's genius are here set in a clear light ; for Goethe, even when embarking upon some literary adventure that ends in the sands, cannot help showering pearls of wisdom by the way, as in the *Wanderjahre* so severely blamed by Lewes, and not to be compared for balanced perfection with the *Wahlverwandtschaften*.

None of the great works are omitted in Croce's rapid review of the poetry, which of course also includes the prose, as all readers of the *Æsthetic* will necessarily assume. Croce is never dull, though sometimes a trifle hard of apprehension, when he assumes his readers are as well posted as himself in the literature of the period, and synthesizes in a few words what they would perhaps grasp more easily in an expanded form. But he always presumes that his readers *are* thoroughly well-informed on all the ordinary matters concerning the problems which he discusses. He starts where the teacher or lecturer on literary history leaves off. And what intrepidity, what freshness of view, to gladden the soul, as when speaking of the far-famed problems of the obscurities and difficulties of the *Second Part of Faust*, Croce runs a pen right through them all, with the remark: "The Second Part of Faust is best considered not as deep philosophy but as a poetical libretto, somewhat in the manner of Metastasio!" That is the true Croce, the painstaking, the laborious, the erudite, who toils and tunnels patiently underground for some pages and then blows up a century of accumulated false criticism with one irresistible dynamic phrase!

Nothing to equal this has been said, since he described the *Divine Comedy* as the novel of the thirteenth century, and Dante as employing it, because the form of prose fiction had not yet been invented. One may be sure with Croce that when he makes statements of this sort, he is always able and ready to support them with elaborate quotations and proofs, as when convicting the modern school of French criticism of insufficient philosophical preparation, he illustrates this by blowing

Saint-Beuve, Brunetière, and Lemaître out of
the water in three articles, where he compares
them with De Sanctis, so little known beyond
the Alps.   Unlike battleships, however, they
settle again.

I consider that the reading of Croce and a
knowledge of his views on philosophy and
literature is essential to a modern education
that aims at something above the ordinary
curriculum of petrified common-place.   Even
where there is dissent, a priceless stimulus to
work and aspiration on the higher planes will
have been obtained, and the great truth
realized, that it is only by toil and sincerity
and honesty in the literary sense, that the
highest reputation can be achieved in poetry,
philosophy, or criticism.   For with Croce are
the failures as well as the achievements of
genius for the first time in the world's
history systematically revealed by one who
has *seen* and *understood*.   Croce has compared his philosophy to a house.   Croce
lives in this house and uses it.   He
says that like other houses which men
build for themselves, his makes no claim
to exist eternally.   No house is eternal, yet
men will always build houses, which are
convenient for the time, and may often serve

to indicate the sort of structure likely to be useful to their successors. The same may be said of this and of those other literary criticisms by our author (which are *applied* philosophy); they will serve the purpose of housing thought for some time—a few centuries perhaps—and certainly afford useful indications for the thoughts as yet unborn, which are to take their place. To criticize Goethe is to criticize the eternal spirit of life in one of its most splendid modern manifestations. And in the case of Croce and of Goethe one may say with truth that mountain calls to mountain.

In conclusion I wish to say that this very able and sympathetic translation is the work of Miss Emily Anderson, formerly Professor of German Literature in University College, Galway.

DOUGLAS AINSLIE

The Athenæum
   Pall Mall, S.W.
    1923

PREFACE

WHATEVER judgment may be passed on the absence of political passion in Goethe, which has been so frequently remarked on, censured, and emphasized in various ways, I may be permitted to say that I consider it singularly fortunate that among all the sublime poets, perennial sources of deep consolation, there should yet be one who, possessing a knowledge of human nature in all its aspects, such as no other poets ever possessed, nevertheless keeps his mind above and beyond political sympathies and the inevitable quarrels of nations. The poet Carducci, as is well known, could not enjoy this good fortune. For when trembling for the fate of his country and surrounded by furious party struggles he turned to his commentary on Petrarch, " Messer Francesco, a voi per pace io vegno . . ."[1], even in the Canzoniere voices seemed

---

[1] " Sir Francis, I come to you for peace. . . ."

to draw him back to the scenes from which
he was endeavouring to escape and to renew
the agony which he had tried, if only for a
short time, to assuage.

During the sad days of the world war I
re-read Goethe's works and gained deeper
consolation and greater courage from him
than I could have gained perhaps in equal
measure from any other poet. This inspired
me with a desire to write down certain
critical ideas which suggested themselves
again during my reading of his works and
which had always led me to a true understanding of them. Such is the origin of the
following pages, which are addressed especially
to Italian readers, but which, on account of
the method which they pursue, may be
welcome to those readers in general who feel
a certain repugnance for the usual " Goethe
literature." This literature, like our own
" Dante literature," is abundant to excess,
but, even more than the latter, on the one
hand it amuses itself with trifles and futile
curiosities, on the other hand, as it is not
governed by clear ideas, it endeavours to
solve problems which are incorrectly set, it

confuses artistic consideration with psychology or practice, complicates what is simple, and strangely exaggerates and disturbs the proportions of the truth. But I think that in poetry, as in everything else, one must go straight to the substantial, contemplating it with an unprejudiced mind, which is also the only way to admire rightly and sincerely; as, moreover, Goethe himself recommended when he warned us—in one of his epigrammatical sayings—" that the True can be found simply," although there are many to whom " it is just the Simple which signifies nothing."

CONTENTS

GOETHE

GOETHE

I

MORAL AND INTELLECTUAL LIFE

BIOGRAPHICAL research is wont to occupy itself in far greater detail with Goethe than with any other poet —and not without just reason ; though it is to be regretted that in his case, more perhaps than in the case of other writers, this kind of research crushes and stifles pure artistic consideration. He who said that if Goethe had not been a great poet in verse, he would yet have been a great artist in life, made a statement which cannot be defended in the strict sense of the word, as it is impossible to imagine the life he lived without the poetry which he produced. Nevertheless, the author of the statement has traced in a rather picturesque manner the relation of Goethe's life to his poetry, a relation which is like that of a whole to one of its parts, a very conspicuous part. For is it not true that the greater number of volumes of Goethe's works (even omitting his letters and his " conversations ") consist of reminiscences, annals, diaries, accounts of his travels, and that several other volumes contain autobiographical matter interspersed or concealed, to which critics are still endeavouring to discover the keys? Does not this autobiographical element enfold and cover on all sides like some rank vegetation those works of his which are more exclusively his poetical works?

As he was an artist in life, so he can teach us how to live. He does not teach, however, as a moralist who sets us an ideal and furnishes us with precepts, but he teaches us directly by his own life of which the observations and the maxims which he wrote and enunciated form the illustration and the theoretical compendium. He does not teach this or that particular technical method, or, if you like, he teaches these as well, but, first of all, he teaches us about the life of man in its essentially human aspect. He shows us by examples in his own life how to solve general problems—problems which arise in the great world of affairs, problems which appear in the narrow round of one's own existence, problems of constancy, of change, of passion, of will, of practice and theory, of different ages and of the duty which belongs to each age, and so forth. His own biography together with his works, offer us a complete and classic course in noble humanity, *per exempla et præcepta.* It is a treasure which in these days deserves to be used to a much greater extent by educators and by auto-didacts themselves.

It is true that a certain literature now in fashion, which shows a preference for what is colossal and mysterious, and which flatters more especially the egotist and the volup-tuary, has begun to recommend the *imitatio Goethii,* describing its own model as a super-human and inhuman being, placed beyond good and evil, and delighting in this repre-sentation of Goethe, which merely reflects its own follies. For the personality of Wolfgang Goethe consists of calm virtue, earnest goodness and justice, wisdom, balance, good sense, sanity, and, in a word, all those qualities which are generally laughed at as being " bourgeois." Other masters, certainly not Goethe, can teach one how to shirk the modest duties of life, how to become cunning and inhuman, how to become sensual

and even bestial. He was deep but not
"abysmal," as some critics of to-day would
wish to consider him. He was a man of
genius, but not diabolical. His words were
simple, clear, and kindly. In order to impress
his teaching on the minds of those whom
he cared for, he liked to clothe it in humble
verse. For instance, wishing to warn us not
to lose ourselves in abstract universality,
he simply said :

> Willst du dich am *Ganzen* erquicken,
> So musst du das Ganze im *Kleinsten* erblicken.[1]

or, for instance, these lines written in the
year of his death to several young writers
who sent him their poetical compositions :

> Jüngling, merke dir in Zeiten,
> Wo sich Geist und Sinn erhöht,
> Dass die Muse zu *begleiten*,
> Doch zu *leiten* nicht versteht.[2]

And what, in substance, did he teach ?
To be above all, whatever else one may be,
thoroughly and wholly human, ever working
with all one's faculties in harmony, never
separating feeling and thought, never work-

---

[1] "If you wish to enjoy the Whole, you must discover
the Whole in the smallest part."

[2] "Youth, remember in those moments when mind and
feeling soar, that the Muse can accompany but is not an
unerring guide."

ing on externals or as a pedant ; a task
which, in the turbulent years of youth and
fascinated by eccentric minds like Hamann,
Goethe may have conceived in a somewhat
material or fanciful sense, but which he
immediately deepened, and therefore made
clearer and corrected, rendering concrete its
mystical and ineffable totality by determining
it more closely. And, on the one hand,
he realized in himself and advised others to
seek true totality in the particular, in one's
particular work, mastery in " self-limita-
tion," and, on the other hand, not to shut
one's heart to passions and affections, but
not to become their prey, and to develop in
oneself ever more and more fully the element
of activity, training oneself not to desire and
to dream, but to will and to act. He knew
that passions, and especially love, come
uncalled for and assert themselves. He
never thought of combating or eradicating
these passions by ascetic abstention, or of
suppressing feeling by over-developing the
rational part of his nature ; but he endeavoured to reconcile both elements and, when
feeling and imagination threatened him and
finally gained the upper hand, he used to
free himself by representing these phases in

works of art : a method to which each one can have recourse, even if he is not expressly a poet by profession or a great poet like Goethe, because this method is really nothing but the faculty of objectifying our mental conditions to ourselves, of contemplating them, of giving an account of them to ourselves, and of thus opening a way to meditation and liberation. Even after he had attained to a thorough knowledge and mastery of himself, even in his maturity, Goethe did not close his heart to the thrills of love, but he never allowed them to check his activity ; sometimes even he treated them as a sort of fever, the cessations of which one should take advantage of ; so that in an epigram he exhorts himself to get on quickly with the work in hand before Love should awake again. As he was armed against natural impulse, he was not seriously its enemy. But he was the sworn enemy of all abstract theories which take upon themselves to regulate human affairs : and here also he succeeded and advised others never to force themselves to follow a pre-conceived plan, but to value spontaneity and to desire to be rather the spectator than the master of one's own talent ("*das inwoh-*

nende Talent ganz als Natur zu betrachten ")[1]
and to allow it to turn to poetry, to science,
to criticism, to this or that material and
species of poetry, whatever represents the
needs and the objective and real necessities of
various moments ("*denn es ist Drang, und
so ist's Pflicht* ")[2] : a variety of movements
which, provided they are not the result of an
amateurish fancy, will embody a much
severer logic and coherence than those which
one sometimes presumes to impose on it
from without. Goethe accepted nothing
from without. He refused to continue to
play the part of a discontented rebel once
inexperience and youthful ferment were
definitely passed ; neither could he agree
to play the part of a cursing, instigating
prophet or of a national, warlike seer, since,
never having engaged in social and political
struggles, but only in inner moral conflicts,
he could not participate with the whole
weight of his personality in the rise of
national units against the world power of
Napoleon ; for, though he loved his native
country of Germany, he could not bring

---

[1] " To regard the talent which one possesses as nothing
but *nature.*"

[2] " For since the *impulse* to do it exists, it is one's *duty*
to do it."

himself to hate the French, and, seated in his study in Weimar, he did not feel in the mood to compose war songs which, as he said, should be written in camp and to the sound of the drum. And because fanatics are rarely spontaneous ånd generally intellectualistic, he abhorred fanatics of all kinds, sentimentalists and " enthusiasts," worshippers of the "superman," mystics, catholicizers, down to the Romanticists. He never lost his serenity of judgment, and he preferred indulgence, not weak, indifferent indulgence, but that other kind of indulgence, strong and sure, which understands deeply because it has experience and prescribes, if possible, a remedy and does not make itself heard; he even came to consider those who opposed him and hated him as a necessary element and a favourable means for his own development. To observe oneself, to examine oneself, never to pause, to prefer the work to the achievement, " *sich überwinden*," ever to conquer oneself; this he desired and achieved. And to be oneself and not to resemble anyone else, but to resemble (he in his peculiar way as others in their peculiar way) the Highest, " *dem Höchsten*," that is to say, Reason and Truth.

He was not less a master in literary life,

passing here too from a youthful fiery assertion of the rights of " genius " and " feeling "
and from rebellion against "rules," not
indeed to the restoration of external rules
and to an aversion for feeling and genius—
since he always claimed to have been " *ein
Befreier*," a liberator, who had taught men
to cultivate art " *von innen heraus*," from the
heart—but to study, to meditation, to
" *Besonnenheit*." In his early days like the
other *Stürmer und Dränger* he had been an
opponent of French literature, which was
intellectualistic and ironical, aged and correct
like an old lady. But he soon learned to
appreciate the clearness of Voltaire's prose
and the value of schools and discipline ; and
he lashed his own Germans severely, who
would not " learn art " and who were wont
to justify every unseemliness they wrote by
saying that they had " lived " it. He also
abandoned very quickly the illuministic
dream that society could ever reach a period
of art and of life generally, in which the right
path would be opened up once for all. For
he observed that the path does indeed open
out as the result of effort, but, like the waves
to a ship, closes immediately afterwards.
" To give poetical form to reality " : thus

Merck, a friend of his, had defined the tendency which Goethe showed clearly from his youth; and he remained true to this saying. The other saying that "all true poetry is occasional poetry" is merely a variant of the former. But the indispensable artistic content, drawn from personal life, must be such as it really presented itself, and not vanity, that is to say, self-complacency, without sound basis. Hence he reproved those who made experiments in order to supply themselves with material for poetry, and, after publishing *Werther*, he was surprised that youths should wertherize and should wish to draw from poetry and put into life what he had drawn from life and put into poetry. For this and similar reasons he was a severe critic of the Romantic movement, and to the separation of the two types of art which then obtained he added as a marginal note the qualification that the classical was "healthy" and the romantic "diseased." What displeased him in the botch-work of the Romanticists was the absence of form and character and the indulging of the ego; and he saw in their "humourism" the acute manifestation of disease, because "humour" (he remarked very rightly) is an element of genius, but can never be a substitute for it, and its predominance marks the decay of art, which it corrodes and eventually destroys. This is a diagnosis and a criticism of a value which is not simply historical and transitory, but theoretical and lasting, inasmuch as it defines spiritual attitudes which are perpetually presenting themselves, and existed then as they do now. And in Goethe's time, as in our time, holds good the criticism he made of a certain Romantic drama which he called a " pathological product, as in it are treated with excessive insistence the parts which have no substance and those which would require substance are, on the contrary, lacking in it " ; and his feeling inclined to lose courage in face of the faultless verse, which had become very common in Germany, where, he said, poetical culture is so widely diffused that " there is no longer anyone who writes bad verse." Hatred for foreign elements or nationalism in poetry seemed to him stupid, or at most antiquated, and his famous idea of *Weltliteratur*, of universal literature, of which he announced the coming, only meant opposition to every nationalistic idea, the assertion of the supernationality of poetry, whereby it seemed to him that it would henceforth be possible for every free soul to seek everywhere its own kindred souls and to receive from all sides stimulus and examples, and also warnings not to enter paths which have been tried already and which lead nowhere. His judgments on contemporary poets (contemporaries of Goethe in his old age) are almost all substantial and definitive ; it may suffice for us to remember that after having received and read the *Promessi sposi* immediately after its publication, he perceived that this book was the mature work of Manzoni, in which there appeared " in its fulness that inner world which in the tragedies had not had room to develop " ; he even noted the fault, the only fault of this work, namely, the unduly large place given to history, by which he thought that, owing to the unfortunate tendency of the time, Manzoni allowed himself sometimes to be overwhelmed, as Schiller by philosophy. Manzoni, in truth, so allowed himself to be dominated by it that he quenched in himself the poet for the historian and the moralist ; this too Goethe had foreseen to a certain extent, when he had censured the division which the author made of the characters of his tragedies into " historical " and " ideal."

On Goethe's æsthetic many dissertations have been written which are mistaken, because they search not for what Goethe thought, but for what he did not think. Thus, seeing that he did not solve or deal with problems of a certain kind, such as those which are usually considered to belong to the philosophy of art or to æsthetic, the conclusion is drawn that he was not a philosopher of art. Whereas, on the contrary, it should have been said that he was a philosopher of those problems of art which offered themselves in the first place to him as an artist, and that here, as in moral life, he is able to provide a great wealth of suitable observations and of efficacious instruction. He was not a philosopher in the scholastic sense, but he was indeed a philosopher in the real sense, in his meditations on the problems of science and nature. With regard to other problems, which we might term metaphysical or religious, he adopted an attitude of reserve, or rather took little interest in them, holding to the maxim that " one should explore the explorable and calmly worship the Inexplorable." It may be (or rather it is certain) that in his idea of a science of nature which in the various species of phenomena should search

for the primitive phenomenon (*Urphänomen*),
which is an idea which can be thought and
seen at the same time, he was wrong and did
little honour to either science or poetry, as
was the case, moreover, with all contemporary
" natural philosophers." It may be (and it
certainly is) that he was much mistaken in
his bitter criticism of Newton, and in reject-
ing the use of mathematics in physical sciences;
another mistake which he shared with other
idealists, his contemporaries. It may be (and
it probably is true, as it is the opinion of
experts) that his theory of colours is neither
true nor false, but physically indifferent, a
sort of mythology of light and darkness,
which is useless for calculation and explains
nothing in a scientific sense. On the other
hand, he made real and original discoveries
in anatomy and botany, fields of research in
which observation and intuition render good
service. It is also not less true that he,
emerging from a century intoxicated with
mathematics, understood and had the courage
to assert that mathematics do not lead to
the knowledge of reality, and that in them
there is nothing exact but their own exact-
ness, a sort of " French tongue " in which
everything becomes clearer and at the same

time poorer, and in which everything drowns its own being and its own character. Original and of great philosophical importance is the idea, which he often suggested, that truths are to be recognized by their capacity for promoting life, and that sterile truths for this very reason are not truths; an idea which we interpret and justify in the sense that every truth has reference to a vital problem, set historically, and therefore operates in life; if it does not operate, it is a sign that the problem was non-existent and the pretended truth mere subtilty, tautology, or verbalism. Further, worthy of notice is that other frequent thought of his that truth is individual and, although it is such, or rather because it is such, is true. Glimmers and presentiments which are slight and vague perhaps, but which foreshadow doctrines which arose later spontaneously, from intrinsic necessity, and which are now shaping themselves and becoming consolidated in modern philosophy.

This splendid moral and mental development, apart from and above poetry, confers on Goethe the stamp which renders him distinct and original when compared with other poets of the same rank, in whom life and thought are merged in poetry wholly and without residue, and if anything does remain outside, it is of mediocre importance, as it generally consists of an entirely personal matter or sentiments and ideas common to their times. But although, as has already been stated, one can thus explain the predominance of biographical treatment in Goethe literature, yet literary history is never exempted from its duty, which is to resist such a tendency and to restrain its onrush and weight, in order to prevent itself from being drawn away from purely artistic consideration, which is its proper task. It must, it is true, ever direct its gaze to the whole personality of Goethe, but with the sole object of understanding how this personality prepares in the various periods the various forms of his art, or how it interferes with the latter, and sometimes disturbs and spoils it.

II

POETICAL AND ARTISTIC LIFE

THE fact of cardinal importance for the artistic development of Goethe is precisely his ethical transition from the restless, rebellious, and " titanic " frame of mind which manifested itself in the early works, in *Werther*, *Götz*, *Faust*, in the fragments of *Prometheus*, and the *Ewiger Jude* to that calm, sober, and harmonious frame of mind, which he preserved thenceforth constantly and which expressed itself in almost all the later works. This transition was frequently mentioned and defined by Goethe himself, as, for instance, in the four synthetic little lines in the *Divan* :

Du hast getollt zu deiner Zeit mit wilden
Dämonisch-genialen jungen Scharen ;
Dann sachte schlossest du von Jahr zu Jahren
Dich näher an die Weisen, Göttlich-Milden.[1]

[1] " In your time you rioted madly with wild, youthful companions, seized with a demon-like frenzy. Then gently, from year to year, you drew nearer to the Wise, the Divinely Calm."

Here " gently " (*sachte*) and " from year to year " and " nearer " are not introduced accidentally, but correspond to the truth ; since one must guard oneself from conceiving the relation between the two periods as a leap over an abyss, which suddenly opened up before him. Goethe had not taken a very active part in the *Sturm und Drang*, at any rate, in no violent spirit of political, social, or religious revolt. His main desire was for liberation from abstract ideas and coldness, for the fulness of life. His chief sympathies were with the sublime figures of history and legend, with the heroes of thought, of passion, and of will. And " mad " (*toll*) he could well call himself with the smiling good-nature of an old man who recalls his youth ; but mad he never was, not in the smallest degree. He who tries to find during this first period of Goethe's life and art a Goethe who is a fanatic or beside himself, will not find him, but will find, on the contrary, much more wisdom than he would have expected after hearing this retrospective judgment. *Werther* represents not a malady, but the recovery from a malady, a vaccination fever rather than a fever after real infection ; in *Faust*, even in *Faust I*, one notices much criticism and irony; even in *Götz* there is reason and well-balanced moral judgment, not to mention the profound wisdom to be found in *Egmont*, which is just as correct and clear in its ideas on political life as on that of the affections. In short, the transition was not a radical conversion or the repudiation of a former self, but rather the maturing of this former self through experiences which were necessary for its development.

Whether this transition was calm or sudden, it was, however, primarily and fundamentally of an ethical, and only indirectly, of a literary character; since only those who are exclusively men of letters believe that it is possible to disconnect the two processes, to divide the spirit into parts, and to form an empty literary problem which, inasmuch as it is empty, cannot be even literary. Nor was it due to external causes, whatever the poet himself may have sometimes said about the effect of his journey to Italy, where so many others have gone, but where no one else has reaped the harvest that Goethe did; "Italy" and "Greece" are not in Goethe's case the Italy and Greece of reality and history, but mere symbols of phases of his inner life; a fact which could be demonstrated in detail and exhaustively, but it is of no use to delay over this question, since it is quite evident to any sagacious mind. Further, a symbol and nothing more is the word " classicality," which is used to distinguish the second from the first phase of Goethe's poetical work ; " classicality " has no meaning here—no true meaning at any rate—unless it is mentally translated by " ethical harmony " or " wisdom." In the æsthetic sense of the word, as that of artistic perfection, complete adjustment of language to sentiment, perfect fusion of matter and form, the Goethe of the first period is not at all less classical than the Goethe of the second. One might even assert (and for my part I should not hesitate to assert) that perhaps he never afterwards attained the pure classicality of the greater part of the scenes of *Faust I*, or of some dramatical-lyrical fragments written in his youth, pages of poetry which can be compared only with the tragedies of Sophocles, the Dante episodes, and the most sublime passages in Shakespeare's dramas.

Thus maturing, when the evolution from the " titanic " to the " wise " was complete, Goethe's poetry had necessarily to undergo a change ; it had to be dominated by the varied moral experience, by the " wisdom," by the balance and harmony which his mind had reached. And this did happen in effect, in *Iphigenie* and *Tasso*, in the *Römische Elegien* and in *Hermann und Dorothea*, down to the *Wahlverwandtschaften*, the second *Meister* and *Faust II*. The visionary and tragical Goethe of the first period has disappeared, and, when he sometimes seems to reappear, as in the vision of the return of Helen to her conjugal home, it is merely the case of a poetical motive of his youth, of which, moreover, he has endeavoured to chasten the quivering emotion, restraining it and making it yield to the allegories and quibbles of *Faust II*. This contrast between the first and second form of Goethe's poetry has been strongly felt and the one form has had its partisans against the other ; but more often the first against the second, and " young Goethe " again became the example and the stimulus to a small and artificial *Sturm und Drang* which the brothers Hart and other critics and minor poets in Germany endeavoured to represent about thirty years ago. The second period has been often called cold and lifeless, and, in short, only slightly

poetical ; but whoever does not persist in
stifling or restraining spontaneous impressions
in deference to some peculiar and narrow,
though high, ideal of art, will never bring
himself to maintain that the poetry in the
works of Goethe in his maturity has ceased
to be poetry, since the wings of poetry, of a
poetry which is doubtless different from the
earlier poetry, touch and caress him in whatever direction he turns in his poetical compositions. In Goethe's case it never happened
that his poetical vision merged in philosophical
thinking, rather, as we have already suggested,
he introduced and preserved his poetical
vision in philosophical thinking and natural
science ; for this reason he even wished,
when dealing with colours, to proceed in a
more concrete and intuitive manner than is
suitable for this kind of research. Poetry
never lets itself be overcome by and merged
in philosophy save in poetically weak temperaments, intrinsically reflective, and only
extrinsically imaginative, such as Schiller
was, with whom Goethe on this point always
contrasted himself. In a letter of 1802 when
writing to Schiller on the subject of conversations which he had had with Schelling, Goethe
added : " In me philosophy destroys poetry

. . . and I never can conduct myself in a purely speculative manner, but immediately I must seek, for every proposition, an intuition and thus I return forthwith to nature."

Therefore all that one can claim as true, in this respect, is the different tone of Goethe's work in his second spiritual phase, in which poetry has certainly become wisdom, but wisdom, in her turn, has become poetry. Goethe never ceases to feel and to express, but he feels and expresses at the same time his own moral harmony, which is the motive in which all other motives, lesser motives, merge. Nor would it be correct, speaking generally, to describe the second phase as didactic and ironical, although he composed in it much didactic and ironical verse, and much playful verse, as befits the " sage," who cannot always conceive everything with the same seriousness or always keep the bow bent. One must only regret that following this path he went too far, particularly in his old age (in the relative sense in which one can speak of old age in the case of a mind which was perpetually alert), and exaggerated a tendency which showed itself as early as the re-elaboration of the *Urfaust* and the *Urmeister* and delighted in symbols and allegories and concealed intentions, which obscure especially the *Wanderjahre* and *Faust II*, in many passages of which we find not a Goethe who is pre-eminently wise and pre-eminently a poet, but rather a Goethe who is not a very wise poet. However, one can determine the greater or lesser degree of power in these as in all his other works only by examining each work separately, and, in general, with regard to this part, there is no further criticism to make.

One should add, however, that the consideration of the relations between his moral and intellectual life and his artistic life, which is so important for the understanding of the development of Goethe's art, for which it supplies the principal historical and hermeneutical criterion, is able to render another service to criticism by showing how useless, futile, and mistaken, in the case of many of his works, is the search for the unity and the unifying poetical motive, in which critics of small intelligence still persist, who are not very sure in their feeling for art, and, at any rate, are inclined to delight in apparent enigmas and riddles, since they have nothing better to do. This continual " *sich über-*

winden," this rapid conquest of himself, which was the rhythm and the law of Goethe's life, was the reason why he could not cherish for long a poetical motive which required many years of exclusive devotion in order to convert itself into an accomplished form.   If one thinks of other artists, inspired all their life long by a single dominating feeling and fascinated by a single image, one can see the difference, compared with them, of Goethe, who was not restless or inconstant, but ever " *strebend,"* rising with a firm tread from height to height and ever surpassing his former self of a short time ago.   From this point of view one should say that in him life, to a certain extent, consumed art or frequently prevented it from growing and becoming mature. Examples abound, not only the very conspicuous example of *Faust,* not only that of the completed *Faust* in two parts, not only that of the first part, but even that of the *Urfaust,* where one can already observe more than one spiritual phase and more than one poetical motive.   Now Goethe, instead of letting fragments remain fragments, or unfinished what no longer admitted of being finished, endeavoured several times (and this is perhaps one of the few traces which are to be found in him of a habit which is not infrequent in the nation to which he belongs) in fancy to give a fictitious finish and a fictitious unity to his fragments and to his various discordant motives ; this difficult intellectualistic labour is apparent in his greatest work and in other works, too, in the last form in which he handed them down to posterity. This is an intellectual process which is very different from that of other artists, who, proceeding from an intellectual plan, endeavour to colour it and often colour with great fire corpses and skeletons ; for Goethe's intellectual process sometimes lent to a group of very living creatures a mechanical or dead appearance ; and it was therefore an intellectual process which was not inherent, but superadded and posthumous. Hence we understand why he frequently did not know what answer to make to questions addressed to him by friends and disciples, who asked him for explanations, and why he got out of his difficulty by means of epigrammatical sayings, which were true and peculiar subterfuges and, perhaps, ironical remarks, not so much against himself (since he could not but know how matters really had unravelled themselves), as against those simple-minded

inquirers ; for example, that *Faust* was
" incalculable " and *Meister* " incommensur-
able." It would now seem time to cease
following the author through those false
indications and to abandon resolutely the
superstitious search for a unity, in those
cases where, in the light of common sense,
no unity exists. When I read, for instance,
in one of the best studies of Goethe that " the
unity of the tragedy of *Faust* is to be found
in the person and the development of the
poet, and is therefore more lively, original,
and comprehensive than any plan which may
have been devised and decided on beforehand,"
I know not what to be surprised at most,
whether at the misunderstanding which leads
the writer to hover between a preconceived
plan and the unity of the poetical motive, or
at his claim to place the poetical unity in the
unity of real life and practice, or, finally, at his
persevering acquiescence in that fiction of a
unity which Goethe introduced into one or
other of his works, perhaps in the illusion to
which he himself succumbed now and then
to the extent of believing that he had thus
really obtained the unity, which in reality
was lacking. The excellent rule, that in poets
one must look, not for what they wished to

do or asserted that they were doing, but only for what they did do poetically, is doubly valid and useful in the case of Goethe ; so innumerable are the fresh pages and the eternal creations which in their constructions are merely artificially held together.

" A VACCINATION fever rather than a real malady " we have called the fever which gave rise to *Werther* ; and now we shall add that this fever is extremely like one of those processes which take place unconsciously in the elaboration of a poetical motive, when the poet seems anxiously to be seeking satisfaction for his needs and desires, and instead is seeking nothing else but art or, at least, principally and substantially, only art. This explains the childishness which makes us smile and almost feel embarrassed when we read the account of, and the documents concerning, the relations of young Goethe with Charlotte Buff and with her betrothed and husband, excellent, patient Kestner. These are matters which biographers and anecdote-writers have in truth emphasized in much too gossiping a fashion, usually misunderstanding their psychological meaning and yielding to the bad advice of immersing again and drowning the work of art in biographical material, by exaggerating and perverting the legitimate ethical interest which Goethe's person arouses generally and has also aroused in us. Biographical genesis, which is sometimes useful to take into consideration in so far as it explains certain artistic discordances which are practical residue in the æsthetic organism, appears incongruous and strange when applied to works in which personal experiences have become completely fused in the artistic idea, as is the case with *Werther*, where the artistic transformation took place so perfectly as to force Goethe even to displease the friends whom he had used as models, who noticed in the ideal characters of the novel traits unbecoming to their real selves and felt as it were offended.

If the critics sin by their excessive devotion to biographical detail, Goethe's contemporaries, who welcomed *Werther* with an approval so enthusiastic as to reach almost the point of fanaticism, who hailed in it the defence of passion and of nature, the protest against social rules, prejudices, and conventions, and even the reasonings in favour of suicide, who wertherized in practice and some of whom, as is well known, were incited by it to make away with themselves, treated this book in another way, in a material way, making it conform to their own sentiments and needs and perplexities and despair.

Werther—" unhappy Werther "—was not an ideal for the poet as he was for his contemporaries. Goethe immortalizes in *Werther* neither the right to passion nor nature versus society, nor suicide, nor the other ideas we have just mentioned ; that is to say, he does not depict them as mental conditions which, at that moment, predominate in him. But he depicts the " sorrows," as the title expresses it, the sufferings and, finally, the death of young Werther ; and just because he looks upon Werther's fate as sorrow, barren sorrow, and its unfolding calculated to lead not to the joy and delight of feeling oneself superior to and rising high above others, but to self-destruction, the book is a liberation or a catharsis. Certainly in Goethe's case a moral catharsis too, but in the book it is an artistic catharsis, effected solely by the power of art.

Therefore, Goethe does not introduce even polemical remarks against the above-mentioned ideas, in the manner which Lessing and others at that time would have anti-artistically desired. Liberation is achieved by making plain the motives and the course of the pathological process, which is tantamount to curbing its power of expanding and to taking away from it the halo of self-complacency and pride, with which it surrounded itself, and the illusion of being in itself something beautiful, exquisite, and almost divine.

The hero of the novel is not a hero, but a being unfitted for life, in which he never succeeds in carving out his own object, in finding his own end or mission. He has numerous habits, but all in their initial stage, all too weak, easily deviated, incapable of becoming co-ordinated and subordinated one to another, and, in some such harmonious order, of becoming deeper and eventually true and peculiar activities. He has a gift for meditation, but his meditation is saltatory, inconstant, and superficial, like that of one who does not take a real delight in converting his experiences into a serious mental problem and in fixing his mind on it with steadfastness. He has a tendency to worship art, but for him art signifies a sort of frenzy and ecstasy. Hence, passionately fond of Ossian, when someone asks him if he " likes " Charlotte, he answers very impatiently : " Like her ! Someone asked me the other day how I ' liked ' Ossian ! "—and his art becomes lost in the inexpressible, and, instead of dominating nature, he allows himself to be overcome by her, and wrecks himself in vague imaginings. He reluctantly undertakes practical activity and abandons it after the first small difficulties ; he decides to go to the war (a decision sometimes taken by desperate people), but allows himself to be dissuaded immediately from doing so. He thinks of the happiness of love and family life ; but, as he does not desire all this seriously, he begins to fall in love among the many women with whom he comes in contact, just with the one woman he cannot marry, whom he must respect, whom he is not allowed to even desire and woo,

As he is very quick in feeling and in observing his own feelings and in expressing them in words, he flies in fancy to scenes of peace and innocence, and, reading Homer, interprets him with the sights of country life, whither he has retired for a time ; and he elevates these sights to the Homeric scenes of the *Odyssey*, as in the wonderful pages of the well, the village girl who carries water, and other similar pictures. Young Werther would have become a great idyllic poet, if he had known how to console himself with art. But the idyllic with him is the clear sign of disease and weakness, the refuge from the command to accomplish some effort. He loves children and patriarchal life and rough and simple work, not like a man who wishes to beget sons and support a family and cultivate the soil, but just because they are distant, inoffensive, and restful things for him who shirks efforts and endeavours to avoid the struggles into which he should have been obliged to enter, towards men and things, on account of his actual condition. He is moved and weeps and becomes excited at the direct, violent, and furious manifestations of passion, of boundless love which knows no barriers, unreasoned and unreasonable, innocent in its fury; he worships them as he worships disorderly and chaotic genius, worshipping therein his own self, inclined to the same outbursts and dissipation of the soul's energy. His feeling for nature is nothing but this thirst for emotions, extended to the life of nature, trees and rivers, mountains and valleys, dawns and sunsets; spectacles to which he unbosoms himself and gives himself entirely, becoming a part of nature, as he already had become, in another way, by his tearful participation in unrestrained passion.

One may even defend what has sometimes been censured in *Werther*, the so-called double motivation of the catastrophe, whereby frustrated ambition and wounded self-love are added to the despair he suffers through his love; but not for the reason adduced by some critics who say that this is exactly what occurred in the case of young Jerusalem, whose history served in part as a model for Goethe (a reason which would be outside the sphere of æsthetic); but for another reason, an intrinsic reason, which is—that a man like Werther had yet to strive to save himself from his destructive passion by some kind of activity, then to become quickly satiated with and acquire a distaste for the latter, and again surrender more bitterly and hopelessly to destructive forces. The readers who would have wished for a single motivation, the lovers of love, the lovers of Charlotte and of Werther in love, regarded and regard *Werther* as a sublime love story. But it is not so ; it is not *Romeo and Juliet* or some similarly inspired work. It is, on the contrary, a book of malady ; and this love is an aspect or an acute manifestation of the malady. If Werther had not shot himself after his last conversation with Charlotte, he would certainly have made away with himself after some other incident.

Although Werther himself is diseased, the description which Goethe gives of him is not diseased. On the contrary, in the passages where the hero defends and justifies himself, the word " malady " is the word which he himself utters as a diagnosis ; his justification is that he considers himself diseased. To the friend who, after Werther has confided in him, puts before him two alternatives —either win Charlotte or leave her—he answers : " Dear friend, that is well said and easily said. But can you ask an unfortunate man who is gradually but surely dying of a slow disease, to put an end to his suffering by a dagger's thrust ? " The famous defence of suicide, which confutes Albert's contrary opinion, this defence which is so powerful inasmuch as it exhibits suicide as a necessary process, which does not criticise itself by placing itself outside itself and its real conditions, is altogether dominated by the comparison between the development of the suicidal longing and a " fever." " You see, Albert, that is the history of so many people ! and is it not the case of a disease ? Nature can find no exit from the labyrinth of confused and contradictory forces and a man must die." As he is diseased, he sometimes breaks forth into puerile ideas and reasonings or into self-interested arguments. When his mother and his friends urge him to take part in social activity and to accept some office, idler, day-dreamer, and passionate as he is, he smiles and asks : " But am I too not active now ? And after all is it not all the same whether I count peas or lentils ? " The prince at whose court he takes an official appointment, esteems him, and Werther complains : " He values my intelligence and my talents more than this heart, which is nevertheless my only pride, which alone is the source of all, of all strength, all bliss, and all misery. What I know, anyone can know; but my heart belongs to me alone." He is so utterly ignorant of the value of tenacity of will and of the importance of going straight to one's goal that he is surprised : " What ! Whilst others with their little strength and talent strut before me, smugly contented with themselves, am I to despair of my strength, of my gifts ? Great God, who hast given me all this, why didst thou not retain the half of it and give me self-confidence and self-satisfaction ? '' But on another occasion he analyses himself perfectly : " It is terrible, William. My active strength has declined to a sort of restless lassitude. I cannot be idle and yet I can accomplish nothing. I have no imagination, no feeling for nature, and I have a distaste for books. When we fail ourselves, everything fails us." And elsewhere : " My diary, which I have neglected for some time, turned up again to-day. I am astonished to see how consciously, step by step, I have come to this pass ! How clearly I have understood my own condition and yet have acted like a child, how clearly I understand it now and yet there is not the faintest indication of an improvement." But the character of Charlotte, wonderful in her goodness, straightforwardness and pity, suffices to prove that the book is not a lyric of madness, but is inspired at most by compassion for a disease.

Compassion : hence it is the work of one

who knows, of one who understands, and who, without being Werther, discerns Werther completely, and, without raving with him, feels his heart throb with his. This is its charm : the perfect fusion of the directness of feeling and the mediation of reason, the union of the fulness of passion with the transparency of this tumult. *Werther*, which, according to the æsthetic terminology which came into existence a few years after its appearance, would have been called and was called s e n t i m e n t a l poetry, is, at the same time, n a ï v e poetry.

IV

WAGNER THE PEDANT

I CONFESS that I cherish a certain tender feeling for Wagner, the *famulus*, Dr. Faust's assistant. I like his sincere and boundless faith in knowledge, his honest ideal of a serious student, his simple straightforwardness, his unaffected modesty, the reverence which he shows and the gratitude which he constantly cherishes towards his great master. I am touched by his tastes, which are those of a peaceful elucidator of parchments, his repugnance for the multitude, for noise and barrel-organs, for walks and excursions, how he prefers to retire to his closet in the evening with his books and inkstand to read and meditate and make notes. I feel disarmed by his small weaknesses, which culminate in his longing to deserve one day the admiration of society, lauded as a scholar, consulted as a sage. And I have not the heart to reproach him for this judgment and these reasonings of his, which are all uttered with phrases and sayings borrowed from average opinion, for how can he be blamed for what is the very reason of his living and working ?

Certainly Wagner is very irritating (although it is not his fault) to anyone who is in a spiritual condition opposed to his, just as the sight of placid and satisfied health is intolerable to one who is suffering from nerves, or the spectacle of prosaic happiness to one who is struggling amid the storms and hurricanes of passion. Intolerable he is to Faust, who, in certain moments, has even a sort of fear of him, a fear of this face, of this voice. And Faust only speaks to him with impatience, repugnance, and sarcasm. One cannot really call dialogues the conversations into which Faust enters with him, since Wagner never understands him and Faust does not hope to be able to make himself understood by such a hearer. But the one only wants to vent his ill-humour against universal falsehood and against himself, and the other is all eagerness to increase the treasure of learning and advice which he has already gained from his master. He drinks in Faust's words open-mouthed, with devotion, although not one of the ideas which they express penetrates his brain with any effect, for it dashes against the barrier formed by his own wise sayings. Faust continues his feverish monologue, in which Wagner takes a part only to the extent of unconsciously throwing in remarks totally different in spirit, which form so many more pricks and goads to his passionate, struggling, trembling master, whose haughty, contemptuous answers again seem to his pupil nothing but a discourse "so learned" (*so gelehrt*); and, as it is so, he does not become perplexed, but admires !

However evident is Faust's disdain, sarcasm, and contempt, Wagner does not notice it, and is not capable of noticing it ; so far is he from suspecting that his own virtuous ideal of knowledge and spiritual meditation has its ridiculous side ; so completely does his reverence for the great man, at whose side Providence has placed him, make him sink and drown the self-love which ought to make him susceptible to these stings. And you do well, poor Wagner, in your simple dignity and affectionate devotion, to listen with deference and not to feel wounded ! For Faust is, after all, only a philosopher and a man, and his cruelty to you is purely intellectual. But be careful what you do, when you resolve to take a wife ; lest, if you do not happen to choose one of those timid silent creatures, such as Gian Paolo frequently places beside his erudite maniacs, but there fall to your lot as a companion a Faust in petticoats, a female Titan, a valkyr, you receive no longer merely biting philosophical lashes, but find yourself the object (and this you hardly deserve) of aversion, hatred, and nausea : as will be precisely the lot of a colleague of yours, devoted to historical research, Tesman, who will have the brilliant idea of marrying Hedda Gabler ![1]

Critics have frequently compared the pair, Faust and Wagner, with the pair, Don Quixote and Sancho Panza. But in reality there is nothing of Don Quixote in Faust and very little of Sancho Panza in Wagner. If, however, the comparison must be made, it is Wagner who resembles Don Quixote, and, in a certain sense, he is the Don Quixote

[1] Hedda : Tesman is—a specialist, my dear Assessor.
Brack : Undeniably.
Hedda : And specialists are not at all amusing to travel with, not in the long run at any rate.
Brack : Not even—the specialist one happens to *love ?*
Hedda : Faugh—don't use that sickening word !
(Ibsen, *Hedda Gabler*, II, 1,)

of the old knowledge. For Wagner's ideal is neither more nor less than the humanistic ideal, joined to the Baconian, i.e. the admiring study of ancient histories in order to deduce from them prudential maxims and rules, political and moral, and the search for the laws of nature in order to turn them to social utility. An ideal which just in Goethe's time was beginning to lose ground, corroded by scepticism regarding naturalistic and abstract methods and by scorn for dry learning and pragmatic reflections, and was substituted or was beginning to be substituted by the revival of the Augustinian desire to *redire in se ipsum*, to overhaul the soul and intellect of man, by the new feeling for the religious mystery of history, by the new rebellious and heroical ethics. Wagner has not the slightest suspicion of the current of thought that is stirring around him and that is overwhelming the breast of his master. He is the faithful slave of the knowledge which is henceforth antiquated. The greatest possessions he dreams of are a library rich in codices and parchments, a closet with many curiosities of nature and instruments for observations and experiments, a medical art which will kill patients by all the rules written down in books, and, for his own appearance in the world, as a professor, acquired skill in the use of persuasion and rhetorical *actio*. The insatiable longings, the giddy dreams of the superman are worries which, thank Heaven, he has never experienced; although (as he says good-naturedly) he too " has had his queer hours "; just as Don Quixote had a little of the world of reality around him in his servant and niece.

I would almost say that the enjoyment which is always renewed when one reaches those pages of *Faust* where Wagner comes on the scene, is only equal to the irritation which makes his master writhe at this point.

> O Tod ! ich kenn's—das ist mein Famulus—
> Es wird mein schönstes Glück zu nichte !
> Dass diese Fülle der Gesichte
> Der trockne Schleicher stören muss ![1]

A person enters the stage, who is sympathetic, and his entrance is worthy of him ! Faust is still burning and quivering after his brief excited dialogue with the Earth Spirit, quickly summoned and as quickly gone. Wagner, who has heard the sound of voices and in his simplicity has thought that

[1] " Oh death ! I know it—'tis my assistant—my fairest happiness is destroyed ! That this plenitude of visions should be disturbed by this humdrum poke ! . . ."

his master was declaiming a Greek tragedy,
evinces the desire to profit somewhat in the
art of declaiming. Like this entrance, each
smallest stroke in the two conversations
which he has with Faust is a marvel of
inspired naturalness, of perfect fusion of
the serious with the comic. The figure of
the pedant was not new in literature. All
will remember the satirical sketches which
Erasmus drew of the rusty scholastic
reasoners, Italian sixteenth century comedy
of the Ciceronian humanists, the polemical
philosophy of Bruno and Galileo of the old,
fanatical Aristotelians. But those descriptions were satire, or rather criticism in its
negative aspect, elaborated with witty elo-
quence, or, at most, caricatures and not
poetry. Poetry is sometimes approached,
but not reached or captured, as in the Polin-
nius of Bruno, who is " a Jove, who from his
lofty observatory looks on and considers
the life of other men, subject to so many
errors, calamities, miseries, useless fatigues,"
and " he alone is happy, he alone lives the
celestial life, when he contemplates his divinity
in the mirror of an anthology, a dictionary,
a Calepino, a lexicon, a Cornucopia, a Niz-
zolio. . . . ." Goethe, however, like every true

poet, will not hear either of satire or of eulogy, either of deepest black or of glaring white. He loves only the play of light and shade, he knows only humanity, poor or sumptuous as it may be ; and the pedant, ridiculed by the polemical writers of the sixteenth century, this pedant, to whom the writers of comedy, in their fury to weight his patient back with all sorts of abuse, often ended by attributing the qualities of a paederast and a thief, becomes in his imagination an idyllic creature, rich in virtues, sometimes even interesting and touching. What do we mean by persons good and bad, virtuous and vicious, wise and foolish ? Such people are mere abstractions, since these terms, taken thus separately, are abstract ; and however much writers on æsthetic are wont to maintain that perfectly good and virtuous personages are not poetical, one must point out and add that neither are the perfectly vicious and wicked ; not on account of the artistic demerit of virtue or vice, but because this perfection in the one or the other antithetical one-sidedness, which it is desired to represent, is a dead thing, an abstraction. After all, who can say which of the two is right, Faust or Wagner ? Who can say that the twofold spiritual narrowness of the one—knowledge which stifles the doubt of knowledge and knowledge which stifles life—is utterly wrong, and that the twofold opposite boundlessness of the other, his mad desperate attempt to unite and exhaust in a single action criticism and life, knowledge and voluptuousness, is completely right ? The Wagner of Goethe, the human pedant, suits so excellently, in his peculiar way, the modern feeling for the unity of opposites, for undivided humanity, that he has had a long, varied, and honest progeny, to whom belong, among the latest representatives, some of the delicate characters which Anatole France is wont to delineate with a light hand, for example, Sylvestre Bonnard, membre de l'Institut, who, before he resigns himself to protecting good girls and to giving them in marriage, also elucidates parchments, with a " magnanimous ardour," expecting from his modest toil the coming of " something mysterious, vague, and sublime."

Our friend Wagner is so sentimental and there is such a sweet vein of tenderness in his breast that his tone, when he talks with his master, becomes lyrical ; not lyrical in the sense of the sublime lyrics that rise and

soar from the lips of Faust, but just idyllic
lyrical poetry, now satisfied, now plaintive :

> Wie anders tragen uns die Geistesfreuden
> Von Buch zu Buch, von Blatt zu Blatt !
> Da werden Winternächte hold und schön,
> Ein selig Leben wärmet alle Glieder,
> Und ach ! entrollst du gar ein würdig Pergamen,
> So steigt der ganze Himmel zu dir nieder.[1]

or :

> Wie schwer sind nicht die Mittel zu erwerben,
> Durch die man zu den Quellen steigt !
> Und eh' man nur den halben Weg erreicht,
> Muss wohl ein armer Teufel sterben.[2]

And, above all, he takes delight in wooing
and enjoying the symbols of glory, the glory
of the scholar :

> Welch ein Gefühl musst du, o grosser Mann,
> Bei der Verehrung dieser Menge haben !
> O glücklich, wer von seinen Gaben
> Solch einen Vortheil ziehen kann !
> Der Vater zeigt dich seinem Knaben,
> Ein jeder fragt und drängt und eilt,
> Die Fiedel stockt, der Tänzer weilt.
> Du gehst, in Reihen stehen sie,
> Die Mützen fliegen in die Höh' :

[1] " How differently the pleasures of the mind carry
us from book to book, from page to page ! Then winter
nights become cheerful and beautiful, blissful delight warms
every limb, and ah ! if you unroll a precious parchment,
all heaven descends upon your soul."

[2] " How difficult it is to procure the means of reaching
the original sources ! and before he has gone half-way,
perchance the poor devil has to die."

4

Und wenig fehlt, so beugten sich die Knie,
Als käm' das Venerabile.[1]

When we read these harmonious lines
we seem to see the partly enraptured, partly
grieved expression of one who is experiencing
a mystical joy and feels himself filled with
a noble envy, the ecstatic expression with
which Wagner must have pronounced them ;
we seem to hear in the apostrophe, in the
exclamation, in the pompous description,
the rise and fall of his voice, so well trained in
the rhetoric of delivery.

The dog, too, plays a part in this idyll, the
poodle, which has followed Faust, and in
which the *famulus* does not notice anything
extraordinary. But, since his master seems
to interest himself in it, he cannot for his
part refuse it a little friendly consideration.
So he offers it the homage of an aphorism,
the caress of a compliment, and ennobles
it to a certain extent by taking it into their
own family, into the academic world :

Dem Hunde, wenn er gut gezogen,
Wird selbst ein weiser Mann gewogen.

[1] " What a feeling you must experience, oh great man,
at the reverence of this crowd ! How happy is he who
can derive such an advantage from his gifts ! The father
shows you to his son, each one asks and presses forward
and hastens, the fiddle ceases, the dance is stopped. You
pass, they stand in rows, caps are raised, and they almost
bow the knee to you, as they would to the sacred host."

Ja deine Gunst verdient er ganz und gar,
Er der Studenten trefflicher Scolar.[1]

Wagner, who is so individualized and so vivid a character in the two scenes of the first part, even amid the allegories, the fancies, and the extravaganzas of the second part, in the Homunculus scenes, does not lose entirely his artistic vitality. With reference to these scenes commentators have made many subtle remarks, which are of very slight importance, just because, if it is necessary to have recourse to hermeneutical subtilties, it is a sign that these representations do not speak for themselves and that their idea (assuming that they have an idea) does not coincide with the form. Nevertheless, Wagner, now "Doctor Wagner," who has become famous, an exceptionally brilliant university light, surrounded by a dense throng of students, provided in his turn with a *famulus*, called Nicodemus, has not become proud as a result of the reputation he has won. He still reveres the memory of his old master and patron, who disappeared suddenly in a manner incomprehensible to him, whose study he has preserved

[1] " If a dog is well trained, even a sage will be kindly disposed towards him. Yes, he quite deserves your favour, he, the apt pupil of the students."

intact with Faust's fur robe still hanging on the nail, and whose return he ever hopes for and awaits. He (says Nicodemus) never admits even in jest that his name could cloud that of Faust, the sublime man : " modesty is the virtue which he has chosen." And when, after distilling Homunculus and hearing himself called " Daddy " (*Väterchen*) prettily, he sees his little creature turn to Mephistopheles, straightway become familiar with the latter, and announce his imminent departure for the Pharsalian Plains with the two companions : " And I ? " the poor man cries out anxiously, feeling himself deserted. " Why, you," the little son of science answers mockingly, " must remain here, as you have very important things to do . . . and you will reach your great goal. . . . Farewell ! " To which Wagner replies, resigned but deeply moved :

> Leb' wohl ! Das drückt das Herz mir nieder.
> Ich fürchte schon ich seh' dich niemals wieder.[1]

Even amid the lifelessness of the allegories, we see his eyes dim with human tears.

[1] " Farewell ! But the word chills my heart. I feel already that I shall never see you again."

V

THE FIRST PART OF *FAUST I*

FAUST, the Faust of poetry, is the Faust we have just seen forming such a contrast to simple Wagner. The other Faust, the Faust of the whole poem, is little more than a concept of the intellect, worked out, moreover, inconsistently. In point of time, the Faust of poetry is the Faust whom Goethe carried in his mind between the years 1769 and 1775; if we wish to determine it in literature, we must reckon approximately (with the exception of a few slight contaminations) the Faust of the introductory scenes, lament on the vanity of knowledge, conjuring of the spirit, dialogue with Wagner, despair and attempted suicide, Easter walk, return to his study; or the Faust of the scenes written during the above-mentioned period and which are to be found in the *Urfaust;* or scenes written down at a later period, but conceived much earlier and resumed in the spirit of the first conception.

This is the Faust in dealing with whom one rightly recalls Werther ; and, indeed, like Werther, he is restless and dissatisfied, searching for something which he does not find in his life, driven to despair, and, if not to suicide, almost to suicide ; like Werther, he is assuaged and temporarily encouraged by whatever brings him back to the sweet remembrances of childhood and innocence (the sound of the Easter chimes), by the sight of the habits of the people (the walk outside the city gate), and here, among simple folk, he feels himself a man ; like Werther, too, he is extremely sensitive to the sights of nature (the moon, who visits his vigil with her tender beam, the sunset). But Faust represents a different tendency of Wertherism, namely, that tendency which we might call heroic. Faust is not a youth who has tried everything and has achieved nothing. He is a mature scholar who has covered the whole range of the knowledge of his time, even in its most abstruse and hidden parts, and his dissatisfaction, his lack of adaptability have suddenly sprung from a long confidence and a long adaptation.

They have sprung from the latter and they break out in the form of doubt and distaste for learning, doubt as to truth and doubt as to the efficacy of truth itself, of merely theoretical truth. Is that which is called knowledge true knowledge? And how is one ever to reach through knowledge the intimate meaning of things, which is so intangible? And above and beyond knowledge is there not the longing for full life? Does not the deepest aspiration of man tend precisely to something which is both knowing and living, substantial and finished knowledge, a substantial life which finds its own satisfaction?

His is a doubt, an anxious search, not at all a certainty, nor a direction which he has discovered, nor the beginning of a new life. Hence, two souls dwell within him, and the one wishes to separate itself from the other. His condition is painful, tortured, it is the condition of a sick man. But how much more noble is his malady than that of Werther! It rises higher and raises its victim to a higher plane. Werther would have been content with a country life and a kind female hand to caress him, or at least he imagined he would have been. But Faust

summons the Earth Spirit with all the
strength of his resolute will and feels he
resembles it. In Faust the crisis of modern
thought is very clearly reflected, when, having
shaken off traditional religious beliefs, it
began to perceive the emptiness of rationa-
listic philosophy, which had taken their
place ; there is also reflected in Faust an
eternal moment of the human spirit, the
moment in which thought criticizes itself
and overcomes its own abstractions.

It is unnecessary to point out the development of this motive in the above-mentioned
scenes, of which there is hardly a line which
has not become proverbial and which all
can go through in their minds without even
opening the book. Our concern here is
to show where the true poetry of Goethe
lies, which, when it has been indicated and
limited by dismissing extraneous thoughts,
requires little comment. Do we need com-
ments to feel the beauty of Faust's address
to the moon, the sad friend who bathes him
in her pallid rays, as he bends over his parchments amid the skeletons and the phials in
his study, and the poetical flight of his
quivering `sigh for living nature ? Or the
spell of the sound of the Easter chimes,

which arrests his hand as he raises the poison
to his lips, awakening and instilling in his
heart a calm sweetness and a peaceful tenderness ? And the merry scattering through the
meadows of the crowd, who, while attending
to their own amusement, make way for and
greet with reverence and gratitude the old doctor, entirely unaware of the lack of confidence
and despair that is raging in the head and the
heart of the venerable scholar ? All these are
immortal and popular pages of modern poetry.

We shall ask ourselves rather whether
Goethe, when composing them, had overcome the state of mind which he embodies
in Faust. In doing this it is evident that we
cannot interpret them according to the idea
of salvation through activity, which appears
in the finished poem and which is chrono-
logically later. In the pages with which we
are now dealing it is not even suggested that
it existed in the mind of the poet. Further,
we shall not puzzle over the various apparie-
tions and later understandings between the
Earth Spirit and Faust, which Goethe may
have planned and of which some traces
seem to remain (soliloquy : " *Erhabener Geist.
. . .*"), but which, in any case, were not
elaborated and never assumed any definite

shape. And later, by a few decades, seems to be the word of warning which Mephistopheles utters in a short soliloquy, against the fatal contempt, by which Faust is allowing himself to be overcome, for "reason" and "knowledge," "the highest attributes of man"; so that not even this idea, which would have thrown an entirely different light on the longings and efforts of Faust, works as present and effectual in the mind of the poet. Goethe, when he presented Faust in the manner in which he presents him in these early scenes, had not yet become a conscious critic of "Faustism," but rather agreed with it; and for this part, too, his true and effective criticism (if it may be called criticism) is entirely poetical, similar to that which we have already noticed in the case of Werther and Wagner, consisting, namely, in the very sincerity and fulness of the representation. In Faust, too, Goethe sings of an agitation and an anguish, and not of an ideal, or rather, he produces and removes the ideal at the same time by means of this agonized representation.

As anguish, and therefore uncertainty, the thought of Faust is stronger in negation than in affirmation, his impulse is surer in

abhorrence than in love. Hence his contemptuous attitude towards the ideas and
questions which interest the *famulus*. A
negation that becomes merry and playful in
another fragment of the first period, in the
dialogue between Mephistopheles and the
student, where nothing is said which Faust
could not have endorsed—criticism of school
logic, of long-winded metaphysics and the-
ology, of dead naturalistic science, of quack
medical science, of dusty jurisprudence which
theorises over ancient iniquities under the
name of right—but all, on the other hand,
is said in a manner which would have been
impossible for Faust, whose mind is not so
free nor his heart so light as to be able to
amuse himself with jests and mockery. Therefore the person who speaks here is Mephistopheles. But who is Mephistopheles ? Not
even in this case shall we pause to search
for the idea which he symbolizes in the
whole poem and the inevitable contradictions
between the symbol and the representations ;
nor shall we enter into the discussion, equally
conceptual, as to whether in the first period
he was conceived as a sprightly spirit, sent
by the Earth Spirit, and not as a devil, such
as he becomes later ; but we shall observe

Mephistopheles too in each episode, since it is evident that in the different inspiration of the various episodes, since he fulfils a different purpose, he is really a different character. Nay more, in the first period the more uncertain Goethe was as to the symbol and the precise rôle of Faust and Mephistopheles, the more inclined was he to portray them in the scenes that he was composing with capricious inspiration or with inspired caprice, without a plan, without any arrangement, with full liberty to treat each scene as he liked and to put into it the Faust and the Mephistopheles which happened to please him at the moment. Here, in the scene with the student, Mephistopheles is, as we have pointed out, merely a good-humoured Faust, well up in the various academical "faculties," knowing all about the professors and the students and their habits, the various branches of teaching, and the methods by which they try in vain to cover their own weak spots. A young novice presents himself with his simple wishes a little like Wagner (" *Ich wünschte recht gelehrt zu werden* . . ."), a little too like Faust himself (" *Es ist ein gar beschränkter Raum, Man sieht nichts Grünes, keinen Baum* . . ."),

and Mephistopheles is highly amused; he
is amused at the undue confidence of this
youth, and the docile and attentive way in
which he listens to him; and, in the form
of preliminary recommendation and ironical
praise, he satirizes the pretentious mechanical
learning of the schools. These satirical sayings
have also all become proverbial, for instance,
the *collegium logicum*, the analysis that drives
the spirit out of nature and deals only with
the separate parts, to which " *fehlt leider !
nur das geistige Band*," the " *alles reduciren* "
and the " *gehörig classificiren*," and so forth.

In the first part of *Faust I*, however, there
is yet another source of inspiration which
must be mentioned. Goethe succeeded in
making Faust the expression of his own
" titanism " amidst the delight which that
legendary figure and, in general, the habits and
customs of old Germany in the time of the
Renaissance and the Reformation awakened
in him, a delight which he felt in common
with other youths, his contemporaries, and
which had already directed him to the study
of Gothic architecture and to the dramatizing
of the history of Goetz von Berlichingen.
Hence the supreme pleasure he took in
thinking out the scenes of Auerbach's cellar

and the witches' kitchen, a pleasure which
still later and much less happily inspired
him to add the witches' revel or Walpurgis-
nacht ; on account of which Wieland aptly
quoted, with reference to Goethe, the name
of Breughel, of " Breughel of the devils."
Let the commentators who are so fond of
allegorizing search for profound meanings
in these scenes. Anyone who reads them
with an unprejudiced mind only finds an
imagination dealing in archaisms, wherein
the early romanticism of the *Sturm und
Drang* anticipated certain aspects of the
Romantic movement. One also notices a
certain irony which permeates it, not satire
or mockery, which would have been foolish,
since the subject is a past which is now
remote, but just a slightly ironical attitude
towards himself for taking pleasure in such
subjects, a smiling complacency. One can
see this attitude distinctly in a small and very
beautiful scene of only four lines, which is
to be found in the *Urfaust*, after the scene,
Auerbach's cellar, and before Faust's meeting
with Gretchen. The stage direction indi-
cates a country road, with a cross at the side
of the road, to the right on a hill an ancient
castle and, in the distance, a peasant's hut.
Faust and Mephistopheles cross the road :

Faust.

Was giebt's, Mephisto, hast du Eil' ?
Was schlägst vorm Kreuz die Augen nieder ?

Mephistopheles.

Ich weiss es wohl, es ist ein Vorurtheil,
Allein genug, mir ist's einmal zuwider.[1]

This is certainly not a poetry that one can place in the same category as the powerful and tumultuous lyrical poetry of Faust, who is struggling to conquer himself with the ardent longing for the unattainable and the infinite; but in its way it is still poetry. Even the personage of Faust was at first tinged by it, as one notices in the initial soliloquy, not only in its metre in the manner of Hans Sachs and in the stilistic movement in the manner of popular drama, but even in certain touches which suited very well the rough hero of the legend but no longer suited the modern titanic figure.   For example :

Auch hab' ich weder Gut noch Geld,
Noch Ehr' und Herrlichkeit der Welt ;
Es möchte kein Hund so länger leben !
Drum hab' ich mich der Magie ergeben. . . .[2]

[1] Faust: What is it, Mephisto, are you in a hurry ?
Why do you lower your eyes before the cross ?
Mephistopheles : I know that it is a prejudice. But let it suffice to say that I dislike it.

[2] " Besides I have neither possessions nor money, nor worldly honour, nor rank. Not even a dog would wish to live longer like this ! Therefore I have devoted myself to magic . . ."

But immediately afterwards, as if he were throwing off a cumbersome cloak which has been weighing him down, and were standing up with breast uncovered, Faust rises to a freer and more varied movement :

> O sähst du, voller Mondenschein. . . .[1]

His tongue is loosened and he cries out forcibly and passionately without any further archaic stylization :

> Und fragst du noch, warum dein Herz
> Sich bang in deinem Busen klemmt ?
> Warum ein unerklärter Schmerz
> Dir alle Lebensregung hemmt ?
> Statt der lebendigen Natur,
> Da Gott die Menschen schuf hinein,
> Umgibt in Rauch und Moder nur
> Dich Thiergeripp' und Todtenbein.[2]

In the great scenes of the tragedy archaism is abandoned. All that remains of it is a thin veil, which, by adding the semblance of something distant and mysterious, increases their effect.

---

[1] " Oh full-orbed moon, would that thou wert gazing for the last time on my agony ! . . ."

[2] " And dost thou still ask why thy heart feels heavy in thy breast ? Why a mysterious sorrow checks all vital movement ? Instead of living Nature, into which God sent his creatures, you are only surrounded by animal skeletons and dead men's bones in their dust and mould."

VI

THE SECOND PART OF *FAUST I*

THE TRAGEDY OF GRETCHEN

ARCHAISM is completely abandoned in the tragedy of Gretchen (which also belongs to the first period of *Faust*). Whatever small residuum is to be found amongst its folds, as, for instance, the allusions of Mephistopheles to the time when Faust used to supply his students with definitions on matters about which he knew nothing, and to the " Doctor " which continued to cleave to him, although his youth had been restored, would be unsuitable and would destroy the harmony of the new work of art, if it were not quite incidental and external, a jest out of place, as it were. Certainly the marvellous remains—in the artifices of Mephistopheles to procure jewels and to bring Faust to Gretchen's room or to kill Valentine or to put the prison guards to sleep and so forth—

but this marvellous serves to simplify and hasten the external and material development of the action and to fix the attention and the heart-throb on the very delicate internal development, the drama of the souls.

The case of girls who were seduced and became mothers, and who in order to conceal their fault killed the fruit of their bodies and were condemned to death by the law then in force, was at that time, during the renewal which was taking place in ethical feeling and in the corresponding new legislative requirements, the subject of human compassion and serious thought. Schiller wrote a rather forcible lyric on the subject, entitled precisely " *Die Kindermörderin*." Leopold Wagner, a friend of Goethe, not without the incentive of the conversations which he had had with his friend, and not without borrowing from the fancies which the latter was weaving round the theme, drew a drama from it with the same title (*Die Kindermörderin*), which is not a mediocre work and which may even to-day be read in several passages with emotion. Goethe himself in his thesis for the doctorate had treated the question as to whether those guilty of this crime deserved the penalty of death.

Several German engravings of that time portray the punishment meted out to the child murderess, and whoever looks at these engravings with their figures of young girls tied blindfold to the chair, feels a shudder as at some horrible sacrifice, in which unconscious victims are being offered up in order to appease the insidious spirit of evil.

In the Gretchen tragedy, however, there is not a trace of a social thesis or a legislative demand. There merely predominates a sincere and high ethical and, at the same time, poetical inspiration. If the character of Gretchen has become so dear to us, if all welcome her as an enchantingly innocent and good creature, if Goethe, in the allegories of *Faust II*, transfers her to the Choruses of the Blest, it is precisely on account of the moral significance she assumes, and not on account of the materiality of her fate. We must contemplate her with the eye of the Goethe who created her, and not with the eye of Mephistopheles, as Carducci happens to do once, when, in one of his fits of ill humour and polemical spite, he describes her as the " foolish girl who gives herself to the first man who comes along, then strangles her new-born child, and then walks into Paradise." Gretchen is not so ; on the contrary, we see the affirmation and the triumph of idealism in a creature who is at first entirely instinctive and natural. In this all her poetry consists. Sympathy, tenderness, fear, reproach, compassion, horror succeed one another and become intertwined in the mind of the reader who follows her fate. But the feeling that prevails and combines all these feelings is the necessity—not harsh necessity, but spiritual and noble necessity—of moral conversion and elevation.

Gretchen is all instinct. Living with her widowed mother, she looks after the upbringing of her little sister, she attends to the household affairs, which her mother who is so particular, " *so accurat*," directs and watches over. Guided by her good heart, she does not spare herself fatigue and trouble, she loves her little sister who gives her so much worry, and on the whole she is content with this modest home life. But sometimes she suffers from it and murmurs against it as against a tyranny, as her way of living and her work is the result, not of a free and conscious determination, but of the conditions in which she finds herself, of her constraint in her mother's presence, of the fact that she is unable to do otherwise. Even her religious practices, her confession to the priest, have this somewhat external character. Her mother and her confessor have taught her a certain childish stubbornness and have armed her with a certain amount of dignity ; a stubbornness and dignity, which prompt her, as if by a spontaneous and instinctive impulse or as the result of a lesson she has learnt, to cut short and turn her back on the first words that Faust burns to say to her in the street. But it is a stubbornness and a dignity entirely superficial and external, so much so that she acts differently from what she thinks and returns home, her fancy filled with him who has spoken to her and solicited her, and in thought she worships his form and lingers over it trembling as over some sweet mystery. In her young blood burns the desire for expansion, for enjoyment, to please and to be pleased, to love and to be loved. Her lonely songs call up episodes of boundless love, as that of the King of Thule. When she finds in her little room the casket, put there by Faust, she adorns herself with these jewels, she looks at herself in the glass, she laments that they are not hers, even if it were only the ear-rings, she sighs at her own poverty and at the poor figure she must make compared with wealthy and ostentatious girls ; and reluctantly she sees her mother take them away from her in order to offer them to the Madonna; and when she again finds a fresh gift, she no longer shows it to her mother, but to her neighbour Martha, and she immediately takes the latter's advice to keep it hidden, and to enjoy it in secret and little by little to display, now one bit, now another, in order not to let it be noticed by her mother and other people. Thus she advances towards perdition, merely on account of the natural longing to be admired, wooed and loved, and to appear beautiful, as every woman desires to be; and she goes to her ruin, yielding more to herself than to the entreaties of her lover and to the bad advice of others; first, talks of love and jests and kisses, then giving herself to her lover, then removing in part the obstacle of her mother's vigilance, finally, her open dishonour and the shame which covers her, the disappearance of her lover, the death which she, almost distracted, deals to her child, prison and condemnation.

The path of love, however, is for her at the same time the path of sorrow, and along this path her conscience, which slumbered at first, because its place was taken by constraint and mechanical obedience, and which is overwhelmed later by the outbreak of amorous

passion, awakes and forms itself ; the outer
law gradually becomes an inner law. Love,
which she dreamed of as full and undis-
turbed joy, not only quickly takes away her
peace of mind ("*Meine Ruh ist hin* . . ."),
but renews and stimulates her religious feeling, which she formerly believed to possess
in the practices of her worship. Hence she
anxiously questions Faust about matters of
faith, and she suspects his companion, who,
she feels, is coldly and scoffingly irreligious.
This first moral recognition of herself appears
especially in the wonderful scene at the well,
where she is talking to Lieschen, who is telling
her of the now evidently bad conduct of their
friend Bärbelchen, who was always so bold
and haughty. Lieschen judges the unhappy
girl cruelly, delighting in the shame which
has come upon her and contrasting her own
careful and much praised virtue. Lieschen is
Gretchen herself before her love and her guilt ;
just so she, too, at one time, who knew not the
power of seduction, who knew nothing of
struggles and sorrows, judged and condemned
lightly, boasting of her own superiority. Now
every blow dealt to Bärbelchen from the sharp
tounge of Lieschen, which Gretchen vainly
tries to parry or to mitigate, is a wound in her

own heart ; and she remains pensive and
sad :

> Wie konnt ich sonst so tapfer schmälen,
> Wenn thät ein armes Mägdlein fehlen ! . . .[1]

Now she, too, has sinned; now she grasps and
understands; and, though she does not justify,
she does not condemn, and there comes to her
lips the excuse that it was irresistible :

> Doch—alles was dazu mich trieb,
> Gott ! war so gut ! ach, war so lieb ![2]

It is almost like compassion for herself, for her
own weakness, compassion which does not
banish the sense of sin. They are the same
words as Dante, a judge but with a human
heart, utters after hearing the tale of
Francesca da Rimini and bowing his head for
a long time : " Quanti dolci pensier, quanto
desío (*war so gut, war so lieb*), Menò costoro al
doloroso passo ! (*dazu mich trieb*)."[3]

Through the stages of this path of guilt and
sorrow—her prayer to the *Mater dolorosa*, her
terrified presence at the death of her brother
who curses her, her torture of remorse at the

---

[1] " How bitterly used I once to blame her, when a poor
girl went astray ! "

[2] " But ah ! what drove me to sin, God knows ! was so
good, so sweet ! "

[3] " What sweet thoughts, what desires, led them to
their sad fate ! "

sound of the organ in the Cathedral, prison and her expectation of the executioner who is to drag her to the scaffold—Gretchen, instead of becoming corrupt, vile and bestial, becomes purified and ennobled. And when her lover enters the prison to take her away with him and save her, she still in the attachment of a love which she yet cherishes, after a first instinctive bound for the liberty and the life which are so suddenly opened up to her again, hesitates and refuses to follow him, as she feels that she no longer belongs, that she can no longer belong to the world ; and when she catches a glimpse of Mephistopheles at the door, her detachment becomes resolute and sudden. Gretchen is no longer of the earth, she can no longer be the prey of wickedness ; she has already surrendered to the judgment of God :

Gericht Gottes! Dir hab' ich mich übergeben!

This last scene is the meaning of the whole. Not light indulgence, not morbid compassion, but effective redemption by the redeeming of a soul, rather by the birth of a soul, where formerly there was only instinct and sense.

Faust in this tragedy is a secondary personage, rather an instrument of the real action than an actor. He represents youthful cupidity, which hastens to satisfy itself, overturning everything in its blind violence. He loves and adores, it is true, but sensually and whimsically, without any regard for the moral personality, which he does not recognize as he only knows a loved person, the giver of voluptuousness, a beautiful form, a glad countenance and sweet prattle. He is neither good nor bad, he uses the least honest means to attain his object, without pausing to have scruples, as the only thing he sees before him is this object. When he hears of the ruin which has come upon Gretchen on his account, he flies to save her, but to save her body not her soul ; and, whilst Gretchen struggles and torments herself and rises spiritually, he remains ever below. If he is saved later, it will be through the agency of Gretchen, through the last words she says to him, which are certainly words of love, but which imply something more than love. The tragedy is the tragedy of Gretchen, not of Faust. The latter is here a rather vulgar being, vulgar in the manner in which he approaches Gretchen the first time when she comes out of the church, vulgar in the artifices he uses, in the seduction accomplished by means of gifts of jewels and the deeds of go-betweens and procuresses, vulgar in his furious passion for this sweet creature. He is not a clever and interesting Don Juan or even a youth deceived like Gretchen, attractive on account of the artlessness of her error, but rather, one would say, one of the many youths or dissolute fellows, who do not know what to do with themselves and play with fire or rather with the most sacred duties and with the most delicate affections, with the honour and the life of others. The sublime Faust of titanic strivings is quite forgotten in the new character, and hardly the identity of the name is sufficient to call him to mind. We might call him "Heinrich," as poor Gretchen called him, some kind of Heinrich or Franz. And such he is and had to be for the greater unifying force of the tragedy which he causes, but of which he is not the protagonist.

Mephistopheles exercises another function which is really the contrast he forms to Gretchen ; the latter, all instinct and heart and inexperience, the former, devoid of all instinct and spontaneity, all intellect and skill. Whether he is, in his civil condition, devil or cobold, he himself knows, and, as it seems, the commentators know. But, since poets know nothing about the psychology of devils and cobolds and only know of the sentiments and the aspects of the human heart, the Mephistopheles of poetry is, in this part of *Faust*, nothing but the expression of the soul that loves and reveres nothing, and, as it considers nothing to be evil and admires nothing as good, it treats affections and dreams as indifferent material, dependent solely on the union of cause and effect, laughing at the beginning, middle and end of a love affair, which he knows and has foreseen, laughing at the process of seduction, knowing well what the end of the " *hohe Intuition* " will be, in which Faust, the lover, delights ; finding quite natural, and a matter not to be astonished or distressed at, that given certain causes, the resulting effects should follow, deception, poisoning, murder, desertion, prison, the gallows. As this attitude of a moral superiority and indifferent behaviour is usually called ' cynicism,' Mephistopheles is the personification of cynicism. Gretchen has such repugnance and horror for him, because she herself, even in her sin, is illusion, rosy illusion, over which passes coldly, threatening to dispel it, this eye with its glance " *so spöttisch*." Thus, in the Gretchen tragedy, Mephistopheles,

whose figure, in the scene of the pact and in
other scenes, vacillates uncertainly between
the devil of tradition and the metaphysical
idea, is human in his inhumanity, and determined and concrete in all his actions, sayings
and gestures.

Just as concrete are the other characters
that take part in it ; the neighbour Martha,
whom Mephistopheles describes to perfection
("*ein Weib wie auserlesen Zum Kuppler-
und Zigeunerwesen* "),[1] a gossip insensible to
anything but her own pleasure, convenience
and interest, and so daring and tenacious in
pursuing the latter that even Mephistopheles
fears for a moment that he will find himself
caught and bound in her very well-woven and
solid net ; Lieschen, jealous, spiteful and
vindictive in her moralizing chatter ; Valentine, once so proud of his sister, who wishes to
have his revenge and die like a man. Even the
personages, whom we do not see, are present
and alive before us, as, for instance, Gretchen's
mother, the priest who takes away the jewels
for his church, or Martha's husband, whose
death the good woman cannot but lament,
since he was, after all, a husband worthy of her.

---

[1] " That is a woman who seems fitted by nature for the
business of a gipsy go-between."

The tragedy of Gretchen is one of those poetical miracles, which combine ease with
strength, perfection with spontaneity, born in
an ecstasy of imagination which made the
poet see everything in its profound reality and
placed on his lips always the right word, and
only the right word.

VII

THE SYSTEMATIC FORM OF *FAUST I* AND
THE DOUBLE FORM OF *WILHELM MEISTER.*

IN the First Part of *Faust*, which was
systematized between the years 1797
and 1801, and appeared in a definite
arrangement in the edition of 1808, there
is nothing more, beyond the various poems
which we have chosen from it and given
prominence to ; nothing more, at least, of
great poetry. There are, it is true, certain
bits of soldering, as, for instance, the scene
of the pact, where the incongruence between
the lines composed earlier and those added
later and the wavering between two diverse
and opposite conceptions of Faust have been
justly noticed ; the Faust who sought fullness of life in the sublimity of joy and torment,
longing to experience in his own life the
peccata mundi which are the world itself, in
a word, the Faust of the *Sturm und Drang ;*
and the other Faust, of the reflective and
" wise " period, who now seeks pure pleasure,
bringing fullness of joy, the blessed moment,

and will eventually find it only in fruitful
practical activity. There are, too, the archa-
izing fantasies of St. Walpurgis night,
interrupted by insignificant, literary illusions,
over which it is not necessary to linger,
and the Prologue in the Theatre, and the
Prologue in Heaven. The first of these,
the Prologue in the Theatre, very subtle,
and, in the exclamations of the " poet,"
likewise enthusiastic and pathetic, is an
hors d'œuvre and belongs to the series of
those outbursts of theatre poets, who sometimes make the theatre itself and the adver-
sity which their activity meets with there
the subject of a play (for instance, Goldoni
in the *Teatro Comico*, or abate Casti in *Prima
la musica e poi le parole*, or ancient Kalidasa
in the *Sakuntala*, which Goethe may have
had in mind). The second, the Prologue in
Heaven, is the jest of a great artist, but
not more than a jest, quite out of harmony
with the drama which follows and which
was, in the first period, planned to be serious ;
a scene in Paradise with the angels, God
and the devil, where there is not even an
archaic colouring, but a dégagé manner,
slightly in the style of Voltaire. The dedication, on the other hand, is moving and tender

in its melancholy, owing to the return to the past, which Goethe accomplishes in imagination, when he opens again his old manuscript of more than twenty years ago, re-reads his youthful feelings and fancies and tries to resume them in order to continue and complete their representation, he quite changed in a world quite changed, without the friends and kindred spirits of former times, who since have died or have drifted elsewhere or have changed too.

The dedication expresses in sublime lyrical accents Goethe's trembling when he sets about the re-elaboration of *Faust*. But his letters and other documents bear witness to the great difficulty he experienced in this work ; how sometimes he seemed to have recovered or found the leading thread, how more often he lost confidence in himself and discontinued his work, and how even he himself considered that the fragment would have to remain a fragment. An " *Abschied* " which he had planned to add to his arrangement, which he did not add, and which was published posthumously with the sketches of scenes which were not worked out and lines which were not added, confirms the feeling, which he experienced, of helplessness in face

6

of an irrevocable past ; and it does not express satisfaction, but rather a sigh of relief at having in some way put the finishing touch to a task which had become distasteful ;

> Am Ende bin ich nun des Trauerspieles
> Das ich zuletzt mit Bangigkeit vollführt,
> Nicht mehr vom Drange menschlichen Gewühles,
> Nicht von der Macht der Dunkelheit gerührt.
> Wer schildert gern den Wirrwarr des Gefühles,
> Wenn ihn der Weg zur Klarheit aufgeführt ?
> Und so geschlossen sei der Barbareien
> Beschränkter Kreis mit seinen Zaubereien.[1]

Therefore it is not necessary to answer the objection which is wont to be made to the analytical process we are pursuing, namely, that in this way one disorganizes and destroys the organism created by the poet ; since the fact is precisely the opposite ; that is to say, that the poet, by a reflective method, has fashioned a mechanism, shutting in and forcing into it several diverse living organisms, to which the critic, by that process, restores their former liberty, without destroying any-

---

[1] " I am now at the end of the tragedy, which I have finished latterly with trembling, no longer stirred by the pressure of human tumult, no longer by the power of mystery. For who would gladly depict confused emotions, when he has already attained to clearness of vision ? And so let me close the narrow circle of barbarous inventions with its magic and witchcraft ! "

thing, since that cannot be destroyed which in effect does not exist and which is a mere supposition, nay even a presumption.

Nevertheless, the theme which Goethe strove to carry out in this re-elaboration of *Faust* deserves to be carefully thought over, as it is of great importance for the understanding of some currents of modern literary history, because it was the model for an artistic error which was repeated innumerable times later, strengthened as it was by the example and the authority of the poet of *Faust*. Goethe intended to answer with a poetical work the question as to the value, or rather the aim of human life. This question was to be heard in all the philosophy of that time, which laboured to set itself and to solve this problem in a manner conformable to modern consciousness. Even the philosophers seemed to invoke the aid or the accompaniment of a poet, who would translate the solution of this problem into concrete images; and this all the more as those philosophers were themselves partly poets, proceeded from poetry, were inclined to return to poetry, and liked to describe their own systems as dramatic or epic poems, not only Schelling and later Schopenhauer, but even Hegel with his Logos, which creates the world of nature, and then is found again in that of the spirit, and is sublimated by thinking itself, with entire self-consciousness absolute consciousness, in philosophy. Schelling was one of the first to recognize in *Faust* the true poem of humanity, created by the Germans. Hegel called it " the absolute philosophical tragedy," provided with a "vastity of content" such as did not exist till then in any dramatic work. Others placed similar hopes in it and, when it came to light systematized, they celebrated it in the same far from legitimate, but just as fortunate and popular, manner, which has become a commonplace. Yet we see clearly what was concealed from the eyes of those expectant admirers and is concealed still ; that the above-mentioned problem was speculative and not poetical, capable of being solved by philosophy, or rather criticism, but not by imagination. Hence we perceive the absurdity into which those attempts had to drift and perish, as indeed Goethe sometimes does, and more so his imitators, who no longer benefited by what there was of freshness, to say the least, and of life in the illusion of the first attempt, nor possessed the wealth of thought and the mastery of art of that very happy genius. Whoever in our days attempts to plan poems or dramas in the style of *Faust*, should be immediately looked upon as lost in the eyes of people who understand such matters, since there are always die-hards and Philistines who think otherwise. In Goethe's time the example of Dante used to be recalled for these poems, and a comparison drawn between *Faust* and the *Commedia*. Here we find Schelling, one of the first, who called it "even more of a c o m e d y and, in a poetical sense, more d i v i n e than the work of Dante," and, after Schelling, innumerable critics of our day. But without adding that, as regards this element of his poem, Dante found himself in historical and psychological circumstances different from and more favourable than those of Goethe,[1] chance willed it that just the new criticism, which was arising from the new tendency of æsthetic and of philosophy in general, led

---

[1] Theodor Vischer recognises this (*Goethes Faust, Neue Beiträge*, Stuttgart, 1875, pp. 133, 368-9) ; probably also as a result of the conversations which he had had on this subject with De Sanctis in Zürich (see the latter's *Lettere ad Zurigo*, Napoli, 1914, pp. 20-30).

to a judgment of Dante's poem which differed totally from the former general judgment of it and of *Faust*, namely, to an elimination of the moral, allegorical and anagogical meanings in favour solely of the literary meaning, and to a treatment of it, no longer in the light of a philosophical and theological system, but as a work of passion, as a dramatic or lyrical work. Hence we might say that what Goethe and the endless train of his followers were striving after, when they imitated and emulated Dante, was the very thing that criticism was preparing to set aside as secondary in Dante's poem; "intentional world," as De Sanctis called it later.

In *Wilhelm Meister* too, or rather in the *Lehrjahre*, one had suspected for a long time a process of retouching in an abstract and systematic sense, similar to that to which *Faust I* had been subjected, as differences in style and beauty between the first and last books, extraneous wedges and numerous incoherences and inconsistencies were noticed : and in the case of *Meister*, too, Providence has ordained that the first sketch of the work should have been found. Just as for some decades we have been in possession of an *Urfaust*, for some years we have now been in possession of an *Urmeister*, entitled *Wilhelm Meisters Theatralische Sendung*,[1] which has come to confirm by proof the results already obtained by internal criticism.

What was the *Theatralische Sendung*? Not the affirmation of life sought in art, of the idea of art as religion, according to the interpretations of a fanciful nature, such as are indulged in to-day; but for him who believes, as we do, only in the "letter" of poetical works, it was nothing but a book in which the author wished to impersonate in a man, who from his childhood has had an inclination for theatrical recitations and compositions, the work of founding a national German theatre. This book is, therefore, the imaginary biography of the supposed founder, of the man to whom this "theatrical mission" has been entrusted, of Meister, and it tells what his family life was, the first signs of his taste for the theatre, which manifested itself in a puppet-show which little Wilhelm set acting, his frequenting as a youth the public theatre and actors' companies, the love affairs and adventures which are intertwined with this life, how he

[1] The manuscript found in Zürich in the possession of the descendants of a female friend of Goethe was published by H. Mayne (Cotta, Stuttgart and Berlin, 1911).

himself becomes an actor and a theatrical manager, the discussions which he happens to have on his own art, the interpretations which he propounds of the works to be staged. But, having reached a certain point which hardly seems the beginning of the "mission," Goethe discontinued his tale and let the manuscript lie untouched for several years. Perhaps the interest which he took in the so-called national German theatre which was to be founded had vanished or waned. It is certain, at any rate, that the book could not be continued and completed, because the undertaking itself was wrong. A "mission," whether it be a literary, a scientific, or a political "mission," is something historically real and cannot be represented on imaginary data. One can understand the *Memorie* of Carlo Goldoni, who fulfilled the mission of reforming and modernizing Italian comedy, and even those of his rival and opponent, the odd conjurer of fairies and restorer of Harlequins, Carlo Gozzi. But one cannot understand the reminiscences of a Wilhelm Meister, who is a mere name and whose works are a mere assertion, or at most plans of works which are said to have been written or about to be written, but which in reality never existed.

And what are, on the other hand, the *Lehrjahre*, the years of apprenticeship, the experiences of Wilhelm Meister, the form in which Goethe, fourteen years later, recast and continued his manuscript? A book guided by a thought superadded to it and entirely different from it : that is to say (as it itself tends to show), that sometimes a man tries his hand at something for which he lacks the true and deep natural disposition, although he believes he possesses it, and in the course of his failures, through false steps, is brought to an inestimable good, or (as the *Lehrjahre* concludes) " he has the same experience as Saul, the son of Kish, who went out to find his father's asses and found a kingdom." Thus Meister, having set out to found the theatre, undergoes varied ·sentimental and moral experiences, meets many different people and passes finally from a vague unsuitable ideal of art to active practical life. In its idea, therefore, the book is a pedagogical novel, which may seem a contradiction in terms, because, although at that time many pedagogical novels were in fact written, these were

pedagogy and not poetry, and were of value
for their ideas and not for their artistic form,
which was altogether disconnected and pretentious, whereas Goethe, who was an artist,
wished to produce art, with a pedagogical
idea, and to use for this purpose artistic
pages written originally with another inten-
tion which he no longer clung to : an
endeavour in which he could not have
succeeded altogether, even if it had supplied
him, as it could not do, with a new poetical
motive. His purpose, moreover, a novel with
a pedagogical thesis (like his other plan, a
poem based on a philosophical system), is
of great importance for the history of literature, because it was widely welcomed and
imitated by artists, German and otherwise,
and was represented, moreover, by some
works remarkable, not so much for their
thesis and their general plan, as for individual
parts. The last work of this kind, entitled
Jean Christophe, was produced on French
soil by a writer whose imagination delights
in Germany of the classical period.

Having adopted this idea, Goethe cut
up and rearranged the manuscript of the
Theatralische Sendung in order to adjust it
to the new plan. The first result was that

the scenes and the figures which he had created received a false light from the reflection of this idea, and the little actress, Marianne, for instance, became a creature extraordinary in her affliction and her repentance, who dies of grief, when bearing Wilhelm a son ; and Mignon was surrounded by a romantic early history, as born of the incestuous love of an Italian and a monk, who turns out to be the old wandering Harper. Where the pages already written resisted transformation, they were given a slightly ironical touch, and the long story of Wilhelm's childhood and of his taste for puppet-shows is put into the mouth of Wilhelm himself during one of his nights of love spent with Marianne, who falls asleep during the monotonous relation of this tedious story. The first books having been condensed (and, in spite of this, they seemed even to the first readers and critics, who were unable to find a reason for the error, out of all proportion to the remainder, and too full of theatrical matters), the continuation was developed in a totally different way and with inventions and expedients in the manner of popular novels, namely, mysterious secret societies, recognitions, adorations of sublime ladies and so forth; all aiming at moral symbolism. And since the same personages appear, transferred into other social circles and amidst new circumstances, it has the appearance of the work of a continuator, of a rhapsode, sometimes even, one might say, of some Giovanni Rosini who is continuing the inspired tale of an Alessandro Manzoni. In the middle of the story we find the " Confessions of a beautiful soul," an autobiography which has no connection with the novel, into which it is dragged in the manner of a shopkeeper, who shoves in his goods wherever he can find a place for them ; a method which Goethe unfortunately used and abused in later works, conspicuously in the *Wanderjahre* of Meister. The recomposition and continuation were therefore laborious and wearisome, and the author experienced on this occasion, too, the feeling of wandering in a " labyrinth," from which he did not know if he would ever emerge, in spite of the thread handed to him by the " idea." But one must not think that this was all to the disadvantage of art, not only because Goethe, returning to his pages and changing their youthful style, rendered them more solid, even if sometimes less rich and spontaneous, but also because, by shortening some parts, he developed others and especially brought certain characters more into play which in the *Sendung* were only mentioned and described.

So that the relation of the *Sendung* to the *Lehrjahre* cannot be regarded as that of a sketch to a finished work (such, for instance, as that of the *Sposi promessi* to the *Promessi sposi*), but as another relation, a much more complicated one, that of a study to a final version, which makes essential alterations in the study, partly spoiling it and partly improving it. What we have called good fortune, namely, the discovery of the *Urmeister*, is not to be enjoyed without some fatigue and embarrassment, because we are obliged to contemplate two similar and yet different artistic creations, each with its peculiar merits and defects, and we are placed, as it were, between two pasturages " distant and moving " ; a large field open for minute criticism, which should penetrate patiently and lovingly into details and proceed to show the fluctuation of the artistic motives in the first and second versions.

Here, however, where we are only touching on main points, we must limit ourselves to saying that, setting aside and in a place of honour the critical digressions, famous among which is that on *Hamlet*, and the many sound and exquisite moral observations, and omitting all the part which is more or less romantic, however symbolical and allegorical it may pretend to be, and refusing to enter into the game of subtle conceptual exegeses, the artistic substance both of the first and of the second *Meister* is to be sought, not so much in the personages of the socially and spiritually superior world, which are outlined in the first books and developed in the last, and which are either shadowy or exaggerated, as in the personages of the theatrical world, of doubtful society and of the poorer classes, of the " low company " in which Meister happens to move for some time.

This is the " low company " in which Goethe, too, took pleasure in his youth, if not in reality, at least in feeling and imagination, and from which he drew his Gretchens and his Clärchens, as he now drew his Mariannes and his Philines. Women who are precisely the moral antithesis of Charlotte, surrounded by sense, ensnared by sense, and in the case of whom it is well to recall the psychological interpretation which Goethe gives of the character of Ophelia, in whom he notes the lustful sensuality of this naïve loving, which in madness, tearing off the veil of chastity, reveals its real nature : an interpretation which, like that of Hamlet, is of moral rather than critical-literary importance, and helps us to understand more perhaps the mind of Goethe than that of Shakespeare. Yet Gretchen dashed into crime and tragedy, and saved herself by atoning for it, and Clärchen was conceived as adoring Egmont and bravely inciting the people to arms, killing herself for love, so that she deserved to be transfigured into a saint or a goddess of Liberty. The women in *Meister* are much smaller, poorer in their affections, in their faults, and in their sorrows, and deserve not tragedy, but sometimes comedy, sometimes the modest *drame bourgeois* and *larmoyant*. They deserve indulgence, too, because they are made thus, they will ever be thus, they have no forces within themselves which could enter into violent conflict and they are not capable of true conversion. What can we expect from poor Marianne, who already has a past full of fickleness and compromises, and who from her throne of boards, from the stage of the little provincial theatre, throws loving glances at inexperienced Wilhelm, just as at all other men, since this is her habit, her function, her amusement? Wilhelm falls in love with her, and founds on this love his whole life, his present and his future. Marianne gives herself to him, repays him with love, at least what she understands by love, since she knows no other form of it. The most she can do now is, seeing herself treated as an honest woman and worshipped, to deceive herself with regard to herself, following and accepting with pleasure the image offered to her, to experience in her heart her regret at being what she is, and to lull in deception her lover whom she esteems and respects. When the latter, after having told her the story of his own innocent childhood and adolescence, spent in the ecstasy of a dream of art, says to her : " And now tell me the story of your life,"—Marianne is silent, averts the conversation, feels inwardly a little ashamed, and is seized with an indescribable feeling of discomfort. She is not at all unconscious, as she immediately afterwards comes face to face with it, of the danger to which she is exposing herself and Wilhelm by these clandestine relations during the absence of her other lover, who has certain rights over her ; but she hastens to chase away its shadow and immediately afterwards becomes cheerful at the thought that she has still fourteen days more freedom, an eternity as judged by her ; then, when the end of this time draws near and with it the danger, she settles her affairs in another way, surrendering herself to the expert hands of old Barbara, who will guide her safely through the rocks of her two love affairs. Of course, Wilhelm, when the deception is revealed, sees his fine castle in the air crumble to pieces, like (in the words of Goethe) " a machine for producing fireworks, which catches fire before the time and crackles and roars in disorderly fashion " ; and it becomes a disease with him. But his suffering is not in proportion to the guilt of Marianne, although it is indeed to his own lack of experience, and it is not surprising that, even after this, he never hates Marianne, but preserves a certain tender feeling for her, and although he does not seek her, always desires to see her again.

What can we expect, too, from fair Philine, capricious, graceful, provoking, wanton, ready to give, ready to demand and to accept, ready to extricate herself from an embarrassing

7

situation without too many scruples, candid
in showing herself as she is, but clever too
in assuming, if necessary, the modest air of
an innocent maiden and a good girl? Of
the two aspects of the feminine in its natural
state (which are, as we know, the woman-
mother and the woman-sexual), Philine
develops only one, the latter, and represents
sexuality in its free state, unadulterated and
untempered; wherefore Laertes, whose life
has been broken by the faithlessness of a
woman, cannot help admiring her. "She
is anything but decorous in her behaviour," he says, "but she is no hypocrite.
And for this reason I like her and am her
friend, because for me she represents in its
unadulterated state that sex that I have so
much reason to hate. She is the true Eve,
the ancient mother of the female sex; they
are all like her, only they will not admit it."
There is only one passage in the later books
where she is mentioned again, and it is like
a lively comment of the poet on his own
creation. Philine, alas, is to be a mother.
What a humiliation! She could not have had
a severer punishment meted out to her than
for the author to suddenly bring into play
in her person the other aspect of the feminine.

But the child (adds the speaker who relates the event) will laugh immediately !

Marianne, who in the ardour, the tenderness of her capricious love for Wilhelm, reveals her good heart, and Philine, a butterfly that flutters from flower to flower and is at bottom harmless, are in their way attractive and lovable. Rigid virtue has no power over them and cannot condemn them. Their attraction ceases only when we meet with other idols of the imagination, other beings lovable in a different way, women beautiful, aristocratic and elegant, like the unknown Amazon or the Countess, who, in the charm of dress and jewels, " seemed to have stepped, not armed like Minerva from the head of Jove, but in all her adornment light-footed from some flower." When Wilhelm sees Philine dancing round ladies like these, kissing their hand, conversing with them and winning their good-will, he feels as if something were being profaned by the contact of this impure creature with the others (here, too, he is perhaps misled by his imagination) who are so superlatively pure.

More popular, but in reality less artistically real and perfect than Marianne and Philine, is Mignon, whom Wilhelm also met in " low

company," in a troupe of rope dancers;
Mignon, the dark-haired girl, daughter of
nobody knows whom, come from far, nobody
knows how, bearing on her countenance, in
her mixed language, in her dress, in her
superstitious religiousness, the remembrance
of and, in her actions and songs, home-
sickness for the land of the sun, for the
country where the orange-trees blossom;
Mignon, who has never been caressed, who
has always been ill-treated and beaten, and
who turns to Wilhelm, who has defended her
and taken her under his protection, loving
him with a love, silent, jealous and unconscious, with a love which is both gratitude
and need for a protector. But Mignon, so
enchanting when she appears, owing to the
very nature of the inspiration which had
created her, had to appear and disappear,
like the other magnificent figure of the old
Harper; and it was perhaps an error of art
to have dragged both characters through
the whole novel, and a still more serious error
to have revealed their complicated early
history, which, in spite of its complications
and strangeness, diminishes instead of increasing the feeling of wonder and vague
expectation which surrounds these figures.

VIII

FRAGMENTS AND HYMNS

IN addition to Faust, another figure, not of German legend, but of ancient classical mythology, formed for the youthful Goethe for some time a symbol in which he lived, namely, Prometheus. But he never finished the drama which he began on the subject of this hero, and of which there remains the fragment of two short acts or sketches of acts. Why did he not finish it ? Perhaps in the very tendency of these scenes one can see the difficulty and the hindrance to the finishing of the work, that is to say, the dualism between Goethe the rebel and Goethe the critic of rebellion. Prometheus refuses peremptorily and proudly to have anything more to do with the gods, to share with them his own rule, or to recognize that he holds it from them, since they are powerless to place in his hand heaven and earth and to divide him from himself, being like himself vassals of Destiny. He proceeds to form his own statues, into which Minerva, separating her own will from that of the other gods, breathes life ; and to found human society on earth, work, property, justice, marriage. But who are these gods against whom he is rebelling ? What do they signify for Goethe ? Shadows of human thought ? One does not fight against shadows and one does not engage in a struggle or in a dramatic contest with shadows, as if they were solid persons. Beings which represent a positive power, which Prometheus opposes but cannot oppose perpetually and with which he must eventually come to terms ? Jove says to Mercury, who informs him, as if to rouse him to vengeance and punishment, of the high treason of Minerva and of the swarming, jubilant human race which is moving about on the earth, that men exist and must exist, that they increase the number of his servants, and that it is well for them if they follow his paternal guidance, but woe to them if they resist his royal arm. As the faithful messenger would hasten to carry back to the new creatures these kindly words, Jove says wisely and good-naturedly with smiling gentleness :

Noch nicht ! In neugeborner Jugendwonne
Wähnt ihre Seele sich göttergleich.
Sie werden dich nicht hören, bis sie dein
Bedürfen. Überlass sie ihrem Leben ! [1]

There was a danger that, when developing this motive, the trembling for Prometheus might turn into reverence for Jove, for wisdom and harmony ; and perhaps for this reason the drama came to a standstill and never got beyond the fragments which we possess, in which we find, among others, the fine passage of the first sensation of death on earth—Pandora seeing her daughter Mira die—and of the representation of death as a supreme rebullition of life and palingenesis, as it is expressed by Prometheus.

From the sketch which he abandoned Goethe took a short and powerful lyric, which is his real youthful Prometheus, not the Prometheus who was to be controlled by Jove and become reconciled to the latter, but the Prometheus who maintains the uselessness of the gods and the power, fullness and autonomy of human life :

Wer half mir
Wider der Titanen Ubermuth ?
Wer rettete vom Tode mich,
Von Sklaverei ?
Hast du nicht alles selbst vollendet,

[1] " Not yet ! In the new-born joy of youth their soul feels itself divine. They will not hear you until they need you. Leave them to their life ! "

Heilig glühend Herz ?
Und glühtest jung und gut,
Betrogen, Rettungsdank
Dem Schlafenden da droben ? [1]

Of another drama also which was never finished, *Mahomet*, there remain plans and some fragments ; truly remarkable is the song which the prophet sings, magnificent in its lyrical flight, celebrating the increase, the spread and the triumph of his doctrine in the future, under the image of the brook which gushes out from the rock, and through the flowering fields, never stopping and welcoming many other streamlets, widens out to a regal river and flows into the ocean.

To the same grandiose inspiration we must attribute various other lyrics of the same period, as the *Wandrer, Wandrers Sturmlied, Ganymed, An Schwager Kronos, Seefahrt,* and the compositions entitled *Künstlers Erdenwallen* and *Künstlers Apotheose* ; where the scenes of *Satyros* and several other small experiments allow free passage to the vein of satire, which we have already admired in

[1] " Who helped me against the overweening pride of the Titans ? Who saved me from death, from slavery ? Hast not thou accomplished all thyself, sacred burning¦ heart ? And in thy youth and goodness, though deceived, didst not thou render thanks for thy salvation to him above who slumbers ?

Goethe, and the fragment of the *Ewiger Jude*, his delight in archaic forms, which we have likewise noted in *Faust*, and which also suggested to him *Hans Sachsens poetische Sendung* and other pieces. But in the archaic tone, which is now grotesque, now playful, now satirical, there are in the *Ewiger Jude* passages of deep poetry, especially in the imagined return of Christ to earth three thousand years after his death on the cross, where are powerfully expressed the painful voluptuousness and the voluptuous pain of human passions :

> Wie man zu einem Mädchen fliegt,
> Das lang an unserm Blute sog
> Und endlich treulos uns betrog :
> Er fühlt im vollen Himmelsflug
> Der irdischen Atmosphäre Zug,
> Fühlt, wie das reinste Glück der Welt
> Schon eine Ahnung von Weh enthält. . . .[1]

and the opposition and combination which human affairs present of order and error, purity and impurity, good and evil :

> O Welt ! voll wunderbarer Wirrung,
> Voll Geist der Ordnung, träger Irrung,
> Du Kettenring von Wonn' und Wehe,
> Du Mutter, die mich selbst zum Grab gebar,

---

[1] " As one flies to a maiden, who has long sucked our heart's blood and has finally deceived us faithlessly. In full celestial flight he feels drawn to the atmosphere of earth. He feels how the purest joy of earth already contains a foreboding of sorrow."

Die ich, obgleich ich bei der Schöpfung war,
Im Ganzen doch nicht sonderbar verstehe.
Die Dumpfheit deines Sinnes, in der du schwebtest,
Daraus du dich nach meinem Tage drangst,
Die schlangenkreisige Begier, in der du bebtest,
Von ihr dich zu befreien strebtest,
Und dann, befreit, dich wieder neu umschlangst,
Das rief mich heraus meinem Sternesaal. . . .[1]

[1] " Oh world ! full of strange confusion, full of the spirit of order, of idle disorder, chain of bliss and woe, thou mother, who borest me to be brought to the grave, world, of which I understand very little, although I was present at thy creation. The dullness of thy sense, in which thou didst hover and from which thou didst press forward to my light, the serpent-like desire, which made thee tremble and from which thou didst strive to free thyself, and then, when freed, didst encoil thyself afresh ; this it was which called me hither from my starry home. . . ."

IX

HISTORICAL AND ETHICAL DRAMAS

ALL the works which we have dealt with so far were motives and creations of sublime poetry, such as had not been heard in Europe for a long time, not since Tasso, Shakespeare, Cervantes, and the two great French writers of tragedy. With *Goetz von Berlichingen*, however, Goethe attempted another species of works, which one might term "pleasing" rather than poetical. When dealing with *Goetz*, too, it is necessary to set aside the prejudices handed down to us by the passionate utterances of Goethe's contemporaries, who saw in his drama a fresh affirmation of the unrestrainable German spirit of liberty and truth and a protest against princes and princelings; a prejudice which still lives on in the stupid nationalistic exaggerated praises of this extremely simple drama. *Goetz* is very different from the *Räuber* of Schiller. Goethe could not breathe into his work the thrill of political passion and rebellion which he always lacked even when he was young and enthusiastic. He read the autobiography of this small feudatory and soldier who lived in the time of the Reformation, became fascinated by the events and customs described in it, and set himself to reproduce them by a process of condensation and dramatization, following the method used by Shakespeare in the latter's historical English dramas. A curiosity for history and a delight in literature which needed something of general human interest to concentrate on, a subject which would ensure a vivid representation of the events and customs of the times ; this something, this subject offered itself to the writer as the everyday strife between good and evil, the struggle between honesty and dishonesty, nobility and malice. Goetz, brave, courageous, loyal and patriarchal, is a sympathetic figure of old, half-barbarous Germany, it is true, but still more a figure of all times. He is surrounded by sympathetic figures : his wife, firm and strong of heart, his kind-hearted sister, solid friends, such as Sickingen, enthusiastic and devoted soldiers such as Georg and Lerse.

Against him are the mirthful and basely cunning bishop, devilish Adelaide, the low officials, the low soldiers of the princes and the Empire. Sometimes with him, sometimes against him, are the weak spirits who know the good and follow the bad, causing harm to others and ruin to themselves, such as Weislingen. As a background we have the currents and struggles of that period, the introduction of Roman law and the rise of the new jurists in Germany, represented by Olearius. Fra Martino represents the monks, weary of the idle life of monasteries. We have, further, the court of a bishop prince, ignorant and material, very like those prelates whom Erasmus satirized ; the revolt of the peasants ; the mysterious popular tribunal of the holy *Vehme* and so forth. Thus we see carried out by a writer happily gifted and possessing acute and profound intelligence the usual directions for what became later the historical romance ; that is to say, the representation of events and customs and the furnishing of sympathetic types. It is well known that Walter Scott, the founder, or rather the great popularizer of this literary species, began precisely by translating *Goetz*. But since this delight in history is not in itself poetry, real poetry, in the true sense of the word, is rare in this drama, and only he who is accustomed to mistake for true poetry something else which attracts his interest can find much poetry in it. Moreover, the present judgment, which many will find too severe, is unconsciously foreshadowed in the common remark that in *Goetz* there is neither a complicated action nor a real catastrophe, that it is not a " tragedy " but a " dramatic spectacle," or a " dramatized biography."

Egmont belongs to the same literary species. But the moral characterization in this drama is much more varied and complex than the mere antithesis between good and bad, which appears in the preceding drama. In *Egmont*, too, the historical representation is lively and clear, in the emotions and humours of the Flemish people, individualized according to their diverse temperaments and conditions, in those of the native lords, similarly individualized, in the figure of Egmont and Orange, and in the personages of the opposite camp, the Regent, her Italian secretary, the Duke of Alba and the Spaniards who carry out his wishes. Goethe, although he lacked political passion, could fathom political affairs with great clear-sightedness ; for this reason he took no definite side, he gladly agreed to half-way solutions, his was the standpoint of the honest citizen, who desires that quiescent matters should not be stirred up, or, if stirred up, that they should return quickly to their quiescent state. The personages of this drama are all in the right ; the people, the Flemish lords, and the Spaniards, Margaret of Parma and her secretary Machiavell, the Duke of Alba and the Prince of Orange, each consistent with his own character and with the part allotted to him by historical fate. Perhaps he who is least in the right is the hero himself, Egmont, who insists on treating difficult situations with a light heart and on disentangling knots with good nature, magnanimity and plain speech. But he, too, is so lovable that, judged by his own standard, he is nevertheless right and, if he lived in less bitter times, if he were allowed to go his own way, he would extricate himself and all his companions very successfully. The Duke of Alba, who, partly as a result of Goethe's drama, has figured since in so many dramas and mediocre *Tendenzdramen* as a monstrous tyrant, we can understand and respect, when presented in Goethe's objective manner ; as

when, for instance, Margaret of Parma
describes him, in the royal council, contrasting
him with its moderate, prudent and clement
members : " But there sits the hollow-eyed
Toledan, with his brazen forehead and deep
fiery glance, muttering between his teeth
about women's softness, and that women
can ride trained horses very well, but are
themselves poor horse-breakers. . . . " *Egmont*
is rather an historical and psychological
study than a poem. One might say that
the weakest parts of the drama are just
those parts (carried out, it is true, with
consummate artistic mastery) in which figure
characters which are distinctly lyrical,
Clärchen, the little sweetheart of great
Egmont, Ferdinand, son of the Duke of Alba,
who admires and loves Egmont, and is
obliged to co-operate in and witness the ruin
of his beloved hero. The scene which awakens
the greatest doubts is the final scene, Egmont's
dream in prison, Liberty appearing to him
with the features of Clärchen. Clärchen
and Ferdinand are slightly unnatural, " con-
structed," not born, both rather illustrating
and exemplifying in the daughter of the
people and in the son of the enemy some
aspects of the charm which Egmont could

exercise. If the remaining personages are historical, these two must truly be called " theatrical parts," namely, in a detractive sense. That both have called forth and still call forth tears is no argument, or, if it is one, it goes to prove their theatrical quality.

Since " history " did not constitute a serious problem for the mind of Goethe, either in its meaning of historical thinking, or rather historical thinking of modern times (this has always been noticed by critics of Goethe, and in vain some critics, like Rosenkranz, have endeavoured to prove the contrary), or in its other meaning of active, or at least sentimental, participation in history in the making, which is politics ; as, moreover, historicity had been introduced into *Goetz* and *Egmont* as a merely decorative element of a world more or less human ; it is not surprising that Goethe abandoned it in all his other dramas. He abandoned it to the extent of showing a distaste for historical names, even proper names, so that in the fragment of the *Natürliche Tochter*, the subject of which is drawn from contemporary French history, time and place disappear, the personages are denoted by common names, such as king, duke, count, priest, governor, magistrate,

8

and so forth. But already in *Torquato Tasso,* where all the names are still historical names, history has dissolved into thin air, as it were, and does not even form the decorative background. This fact has given rise to the wrong judgment, especially on the part of Italian readers, that this drama is a poor creation ; whereas, one should rather assert that in *Tasso,* wherever the decoration is least, the prominence given to thought and passion is all the greater. But those readers who have accused it of coldness are not entirely wrong. It is similar in tenor to *Egmont* : the psychological study of a character or a situation, but not the complete possession on the part of the poet of this character or situation, towards which he adopts a serene, inquiring and critical attitude. Goethe's Torquato has been compared to Werther. But in *Werther* we have that combination of sympathizing with passion and dominating it at the same time, which is the peculiar province of poetry, whereas in *Tasso* the inspiring muse should be the understanding, discerning and critical mind, which, it is true, fulfils a high function, but for this very reason can never fulfil the function of an inspiring muse. In the character of Torquato, the poet is not worshipped as an overbearing, boundless genius, dashing against and uprooting the dykes of practical life, or beating against them, wounding himself and perishing as a man. Such a worship of the poet became afterwards characteristic of the Romantic movement, and was reflected in innumerable novels, dramas and pictures. Possibly this motive was Goethe's first motive ; we seem to trace it in the first scenes of the drama. But as was usual with Goethe, this corresponding mental state was rapidly overcome. The first motive was toned down in the following scenes and throughout the rest of the drama, not, however, without leaving a certain inconsistency and discord. Torquato Tasso appears in the course of this drama, as he does in biography, as a diseased man : diseased, it is true, as a reaction from his own extreme vitality as a poet, yet diseased. And thus he is represented with fine psychological analysis, or rather psychopathological analysis. All who come in touch with him regard him and treat him as such and vainly endeavour to cure him. Duke Alphonso, a man of moderation, grave Antonio Montecatino (who at first appears to be wrong and then turns out to be right, and excessively so), the knowing and not entirely disinterested Leonora Sanvitale, Princess Eleonora herself, who loves him and does not succeed in calming the tempests of his emotions, not even in curbing their external and visible excesses. Among other peculiarities, one characteristic is his hallucination of persecution which Goethe depicts with great realism, studying its beginning, its temporary subsiding and its more violent outbreak, as Tasso becomes more and more suspicious of his surroundings. The result is a work which can be praised to excess or blamed to excess according as it is considered from the one or the other point of view, namely, as a work of psychological description or as a poetical work. Certainly in *Torquato Tasso* much more easily than the actions and passions can one call to mind the moral characters and the sayings in which they express themselves, as :

> Es bildet ein Talent sich in der Stille,
> Sich ein Charakter in dem Strom der Welt ;[1]

or :

> Der Mässige wird öfters kalt genannt
> Von Menschen, die sich warm vor andern glauben,
> Weil sie die Hitze fliegend überfällt.[2]

[1] " A talent is formed in calm surroundings, a character in the torrent of the world."

[2] " A moderate man is often called ' cold ' by people, who think themselves ' warmer ' than others, because a passing fire inspires them."

or Antonio's praise of Ariosto's poetry, or
Princess Eleonora's description of the heart
of women and of their sense of what "*sich
ziemt.*" These are delicate thoughts, deli-
cately expressed.

There is far more powerful emotion in
Iphigenie, which also consists of psychological
analysis and moral reflection, and which for
this very reason is not Greek and still less
primitive, certainly, although on the surface
it may appear to be, not more so than
Racine's *Phèdre* or Alfieri's *Mirra*. The
emotion centres in the person of Iphigenie,
who is the embodiment of moral purity and
truthfulness and who triumphs solely by
virtue of this purity and truthfulness.
Iphigenie, priestess of Artemis, but in reality
a Christian nun and saint, who herself puts
an end to the long criminal fate which has
burdened her family, the race of the Atridae,
restores peace of mind to her brother, who has
been tormented by the Furies, and opens up
before him a new life. This she achieves,
not by external or magical means, such as the
stealing of the image entrusted to her and
other similar methods, but by spiritual
efficacy and inner purification. Thus she
cannot follow to the end the path traced for

her by Pylades, the man who is entirely given up to his profession as a warrior and politician. She is arrested or held back by a sense of contradiction, as it were, which develops in her mind between the means and the end. This is her dramatic struggle ; a terrible conflict arises in her heart. An inner voice holds her back ; but the voice of Pylades, who incites her, is very authoritative and speaks seriously :

> Das Leben lehrt uns, weniger mit uns
> Und andern strenge zu sein ; du lernst es auch.
> So wunderbar ist dies Geschlecht gebildet,
> So vielfach ist's verschlungen und verknüpft
> Dass keiner in sich selbst, noch mit den andern
> Sich rein und unverworren halten kann.
> Auch sind wir nicht bestellt uns selbst zu richten ;
> Zu wandeln und auf seinen Weg zu sehen
> Ist eines Menschen erste nächste Pflicht ;
> Denn selten schätzt er recht was er gethan,
> Und was er thut, weiss er fast nie zu schätzen.[1]

If she is not carried away by these words, it is because her inner voice is not a superficial

[1] " Life teaches us to be less severe with ourselves and with others ; you will learn it too. This human race is so strangely formed, so variously intertwined and joined together, that no one can preserve himself pure and without inconsistency in himself and with regard to others. Nor are we allowed to judge ourselves : the first and most important duty of a man is to go forward and watch his own path ; for seldom does he judge rightly what he has done ; and what he is doing, he can hardly ever judge."

reasoner and resists arguments, even those which she might attempt herself :

Ich untersuche nicht, ich fühle nur.[1]

And Iphigenie finds in the categorical imperative of truthfulness, which implies at the same time justice to others, the strength to convince others and to obtain their voluntary and complete consent, thus completing her work of salvation without staining it with a lie or an injustice.

Iphigenie is the " eternal feminine," which appears moreover in Princess Eleonora in *Tasso*, and reappears finally in the words which form the conclusion of *Faust II* : the feminine, which is not effeminacy or mere womanliness, but pure morality, which has decisive value in the full affirmation of human liberty. Instead of the idea of " sister," such as interpreters attribute to her, she might with greater justice be called, theologically, the Virgin Mary, co-redemptress of man, to whom merely his robust will, which pursues its own particular aim, is not a sufficient or unerring guide. Yet, however much, when we think of her, we may be reminded of this and other matters, Goethe's

[1] " I question not, I only feel."

Iphigenie is not an idea or a type, but a person : one of those sweet creatures who have accumulated an infinite amount of moral energy, partly because, having touched death, they have received the Eternal into their hearts forever, and are dead to the world, to the material and superficial world :

> Selbst gerettet, war
> Ich nun ein Schatten mir, und frische Lust
> Des Lebens blüht in mir nicht wieder auf.[1]

Their lack of joy and life is alone capable of bringing back both joy and life to a languishing and disheartened world.

[1] " Even when saved, I seemed to myself a shadow, and the fresh joy of life will never again blossom within me."

X

HELENA

THE figures of myth and ancient art, when they become a reality in our minds, continue there their life even apart from the settings of the original tales and dramas : they become deeper and broader, they enrich themselves with our thoughts, emotions and impressions, without losing their primitive traits. It is a spiritual process different, not essentially but in a certain degree, from that process whereby we use ancient names and some features of the personages and some actions to express our feelings, altering their real features and delighting in changing them freely, preserving of them only an evanescent contour, sufficient for our artistic purpose. Goethe, who had adopted the latter method in *Faust*, *Prometheus*, and in the fragments of the *Ewiger Jude* and *Mahomet*, attempted the first method in *Achilleïs*, which was never finished, and in 1800 he wrote the lines of *Helena*. This second method presupposes a keen historical sense, which grasps the essential quality of ancient poetry and endeavours to fathom the spirit of its various forms ; and under the influence of the growth of historical study during the following periods, many artists turned to it and derived various inspiration from it. Goethe, however, was here, too, among the first, or rather the first.

The Helena of Goethe is indeed the " fatal Helen " of the ancients, the peerless beauty for whom the heroes of Greece and Asia fought ten years, sacrificing their bodies as if for a sacred hecatomb ; the Helen whom Greeks and Trojans alike worshipped, as a portent, as it were, and for whom they were willing to risk and lose their lives ; the Helen before whom bowed the old men of the Scæan gates, doing honour to the divine gift of beauty which her whole form embodied ; the Helen who was finally brought back, after countless struggles and vicissitudes, to the royal palace of Sparta, like some image that had been carried off and reconquered.

At the same time, however, she is a conception of Goethe, which, although it

seems to have been drawn from the heart of
the ancient myth, is intrinsically something
new and modern, like Goethe's conception
of Iphigenie.   It is Beauty, enchantment,
intoxication, perdition; Beauty, the very
presence of which causes a trembling, a
desire for joy, a desire for death, innocently
guilty in this effect which it produces, yet
seized by the sense of the guilt of which it
is not guilty, and awaiting it knows not
what punishment, which will put an end
to its tempestuous, devastating career.   This
Beauty, on account of the power it displays,
is heroic ; this sense of guilt, combined with
the sense of the necessity which transcends
it, is tragic.   In the human individual, who
bears the fatal gift and awaits the fatal
punishment, a cosmic mystery is being fulfilled.   Hence nothing individual or personal
is mingled with the emotion of the individual,
but individuality itself is raised to the height
of this mystery and becomes impassable and
heroic.

Is it a Greek tragedy we are reading, when
we see Helen before us, who, arriving at the
royal palace of Sparta, begins to speak as if
in a dream, recalling her own fate ?   This
appearance is introduced and maintained, in

spite of the German verse ; a proof that the poet really had his mind full of classical antiquity when commencing his song, which expresses and suggests so many things which no ancient poet could have either expressed or suggested, since they had not yet accumulated in his conscience.

> Bewundert viel und viel gescholten Helena
> Vom Strande komm' ich. . . .[1]

This Helen, greatly admired and greatly blamed, comes to us moderns from the fulness of our memories, from the wealth of the classical world which constitutes the basis of our own history. And with her, who comes back from such colossal adventures, we, before the royal palace of Sparta, return that moment in thought to her father's house, to her childhood, her marriage, to distant things, since which—as she murmurs to herself :

> Ist viel geschehen, was die Menschen weit und breit
> So gern erzählen, aber der nicht gerne hört
> Von dem die Sage wachsend sich zum Märchen spann.[2]

It is a Helen, who is already conscious of

---

[1] " Greatly admired and greatly blamed Helen, from the shore I come. . . ."

[2] " Much has happened which men far and wide love to talk of, but which he does not care to hear who has seen his legend growing around him and weaving itself into a tale."

belonging to legend, to a legend which causes
her sadness, rather than pride. Her human
flesh suffers while fulfilling the mission
assigned to her.

Her consort and king has made her precede
him from the shore with her handmaidens,
the Trojan captives. She hesitates uncertainly ; she has a presentiment of something
grave and cruel which is to happen. She
knows not whether she returns as a consort
and queen or as something conquered, as a
prisoner, as a victim destined to avenge the
long sorrows sustained by the Greeks. She
only knows that her fame and her fate have
to proceed through the double vicissitude of
glory and malediction, of triumph and condemnation, such as is the sad accompaniment
of Beauty :

Denn Ruf und Schicksal bestimmten fürwahr die Unster-
    blichen
Zweideutig mir, der Schöngestalt bedenkliche
Begleiter, die an dieser Schwelle mir sogar
Mit düster drohender Gegenwart zur Seite stehn.[1]

The king seldom glanced at her during their
voyage, he never spoke a kind word to her,
as if he were pondering on the sentence to

---

[1] " For in truth the Immortals allotted to me ambiguously
fame and fate, the dangerous companions of beauty, and
even on this threshold they stand beside me with their
dark, threatening presence."

be meted out to her ; and, when they reached land, he ordered her to precede him and prepare a sacrifice. This sets her thinking, but does not disturb her or agitate her, for she puts everything into the hands of the gods, who alone allot what mortals bear. Yet she hesitates when entering her old home, which in memory she has so often revisited and longed for and despaired of ever seeing again : and now she stands before it and her feet no longer carry her willingly up the steep steps, down which she skipped gaily as a child. When she enters the hall, she is terrified at the emptiness which she feels around her and at noticing a mysterious female form, crouching near the hearth : and she draws back irresolute. She is terrified, yet she knows that she, daughter of Jove, must not fear. But she also knows that fear can sometimes shake even the breast of heroes :

Der Tochter Zeus geziemet nicht gemeine Furcht
Und flüchtig-leise Schreckenshand berührt sie nicht ;
Doch das Entsetzen, das dem Schoss der alten Nacht
Von Urbeginn entsteigend, vielgestaltet noch
Wie glühende Wolken, aus des Berges Feuerschlund,
Herauf sich wälzt, erschüttert auch des Helden Brust.[1]

[1] "Vulgar fear does not befit the daughter of Jove, and the light, passing hand of terror does not touch her. But the horror which, rising from the womb of ancient night, assumes many shapes like fiery clouds bursting forth from the jaws of a volcano, shakes even the breast of a hero."

The old woman's form, seated and motionless, whom Helen at first takes to be the stewardess, of whom the king has told her and to whom she imparts orders which are taken no notice of, is a Phorkyas, who engages in a bitter contest of words with Helen's handmaidens ; and she recapitulates in questioning fashion to Helen, who has held herself aloof from this quarrel, reproving them, mistress as she is of both parties, the latter's terrible past, all the men whom she has fascinated, all the men to whom she has belonged ; and finally she tells her that the sacrifice now being prepared will have her for its victim, that for her are the tripod, the bowl and the sharpened axe.

At this point, however, the powerful fragment of poetry, written in 1800 and subsequently retouched and extended here and there, is followed by the symbolical transition from Helen to Faust, from the Greek world to the mediæval and Teutonic world, with the union of both ; and the Phorkyas reveals herself as Mephistopheles. The poetry becomes gradually more superficial on account of the allegorizing on the one hand, and of the operatic scenography on the other. This is not the place to deal with this part of the poem which, being of later date, is utterly foreign to the first poetical composition which treats of the reappearance of Helen. It belongs to *Faust II*.

XI

HERMANN UND DOROTHEA

WE have seen how thoroughly Goethe imbibed and assimilated ancient art and literature. But in *Hermann und Dorothea,* which his compatriots never weary of acclaiming as the introduction of the Homeric element into German poetry, the raising of the latter to pure Hellenic art and, as it were, the consummation of the marriage of Helen and Faust, Goethe adopts towards classic art another attitude, a more genial one. He contemplates classical forms as they are and, since classical forms, as mere forms, are empty, he amuses himself with embellishing them with a new content. This does not imply that *Hermann und Dorothea* is not, within its own limits, a charming poem, but merely that it is necessary to resign oneself to this fact and to consider the poem as it is in reality.

The importance of this poem was exaggerated from the time it appeared on account of the great task that had just been accomplished at that time in Germany in the matter of Greek sculpture by the work of Winckelmann and his school, of the great work, closely connected with this, on the poetry of Homer, and of the rather fantastic and arbitrary æsthetic canons deduced from these, which had engendered the expectation of some Olympian or divine art, which was to be rediscovered in modern times by the efforts of German genius. The solemn document expressing this expectation and the consequent over-estimation of Goethe's poem is the very long and in many respects very beautiful treatise, entitled *Über Hermann und Dorothea*, of Wilhelm von Humboldt, who thought he could prove that this artistic composition " appropriates to itself the general nature of Poetry and of Art in a purer fashion than one could easily find in any other work of art " ; and he praised its entirely Homeric " objectivity," and he discovered in it similarity of style with the " style of the figurative arts," and he hailed it as the only work which deserved to be placed side by side with those of the

" ancients." Yet the fact that Goethe's predecessor and guide in this conception and in this style was a philologist and translator of Homer, namely, Voss in his *Luise*, ought to have sufficed to put him on the right path of judgment and remove the veil which interposed itself between his vision and the work.

In addition to the enthusiasm of philologists and men of letters there was on this occasion the enthusiasm of good people, of the honest bourgeois, of mothers, girls and old maids, schoolmasters (and this is the famous alliance which German critics maintain has been formed in this poem between the *deutsches Herz* and the *antike Kunst !*), who all found in it what they deeply desired and admired : a display of very honest sentiments and good works, love which immediately becomes a bethrothal, the anxiety of parents for the happiness of their children, the obedience of children which does not exclude independence when it fixes on what is right, and finally agrees substantially with the wish of the parents, virtue which is unfortunate and rewarded, and a rich collection of remarks and maxims of the kind one accepts with the remark : That's true—

without much effort of meditation and without having to overcome the surprise of the apparent paradox. It is the luck which Hegel once said philosophers have not and preachers have in abundance, that the latter satisfy and rouse to edification immediately, because they repeat things of which their hearers are already convinced and with which they are familiar. As I write I am reminded of an old German lady, who taught me when a boy and who made me read *Hermann und Dorothea*. From time to time her eyes were dim with tears and she sighed with compassion. Good things, after all, which one can joke about, but the respectability and worth of which we do not intend to question.

Neither Goethe nor Voss, however, made any real innovation by clothing the material of domestic life in hexameters with Homeric turns and touches ; because for a long time (since the Renaissance and even much earlier) these exercises had been in vogue, adorning the humble everyday affairs and tales of modern times with the garb of Cicero and Virgil according to the subject in question. Even now, such is the decay of the Latin language, certain people take delight in similar productions. *Hermann und Dorothea* was translated into Latin, an effort which would not have been possible in the case of *Faust* or *Werther*. This rendering, which was a kind of repayment, pleased Goethe immensely, to whom his mediocre work was ever dear, because the re-reading of it must indeed have filled him with a certain complacency, not unaccompanied by a smile.

In order to achieve such artistic works as these, a subject should be selected which shall not too deeply engage thought and feeling, and which shall not express itself in emotional or direct form. Hence the tale of *Hermann und Dorothea* is the most obvious and simple story possible. An honest marriageable youth, whom his parents wish to see married, going out to see a crowd of war refugees pass along the high road, falls in love with a good and beautiful marriageable girl, who is amongst them, and, after a short hesitation on the part of the parents on account of this adventure, marries her with their consent and to the satisfaction of all. It is a tale of which, from the very first touches, one can foresee not only the end, but even the course. The " typical element " in the action and in the characters, which seems to paralyse to such an extent certain critics (who are not all poor critics, since we find Scherer among their number), who contrast it favourably with the individual and realistic element in the youthful works of Goethe, is here not even the expression of a calm soul and a philosophic mind, but is rather the mark of the poet's relative lack of interest in these incidents and characters, so intent is he on the phrase, the rhythm and the metre, by which chiefly he desires to obtain his peculiar artistic effect.

In the works of his youth, we find a very different kind of Homeric element, the eternal Homer, which is also fresh and direct poetry ; and there it is also to be found in its idyllic form, as anyone will admit who remembers a few pages of *Werther*. And whoever recalls some other German books of the same period, for example, the autobiography of Jung Stilling, especially the passage where he relates his childhood and the story of his family, will see what *Hermann und Dorothea* would have been, if Goethe had felt it directly. In Jung Stilling, too, one reads about domestic occurrences, betrothals and weddings, and rustic nuptial feasts are described ; and the manner sometimes seems to approach that of Voss and Goethe :

After they had all eaten and drunk their fill, sensible conversations were begun. But William and his bride wished to be alone and to talk ; therefore, they went further into the forest. With the distance from the others their love grew. Ah, if there did not exist the needs of life, if there were no cold, frost, or rain, what could this pair have lacked as far as earthly bliss was concerned ? The two old fathers, who in the meantime had sat down together with a jug of beer, began a serious conversation.

In Jung Stilling too there is a Dorothea, *Dörtchen,* an honest maiden married to an honest youth ; but how differently she touches our hearts ! She marries and dies young ; some months before her death she begins to decline, she knows not why, and has a presentiment of her death and confides in her husband :

Oh no, I am not out of humour, dearest ! I am not discontented. I love you, I love our parents and sisters, yes, I love all men and women. But I want to tell you what I feel. When I see in spring how everything opens out, the leaves on the trees, the flowers and grasses, I feel as if it doesn't touch me, I then feel as if I were in a world to which I do not belong. But as soon as I see a yellow leaf, a faded flower or dried grass, then tears burst forth and I feel so happy, so utterly happy that I can't express it ; and yet I am never joyful over it. Formerly all this used to sadden me and I never felt happier than in spring.

And when some time after her death her widowed husband with his little son, returning to a spot where in happier days they had

made an excursion into the country with
Dorothea, find the little knife which she had
lost there and searched for in vain, what
distressing lamentations !

After this, having had a good weep, we
too enjoy the learned and pleasant play of
Goethe's hexameters and become enraptured
with Humboldt over the little pictures which
the artist draws :

Als ich nun meines Weges die neue Strasse hinanfuhr,
Fiel mir ein Wagen ins Auge, von tüchtigen Bäumen
   gefüget,
Von zwei Ochsen gezogen, den grössten und stärksten
   des Auslands ;
Nebenher aber ging mit starken Schritten ein Mädchen,
Lenkte mit langem Stabe die beiden gewaltigen Thiere,
Trieb sie an und hielt sie zurück, sie leitete klüglich.[1]

" One seems to see (says Humboldt) one of
the tall figures that one admires sometimes in
the works of the ancients, on carved stones."
Yes, and also in outlined engravings, in
certain statues and bas-reliefs, in certain
paintings, which pleased the art of the period,
according to the academical-imperial good
taste, which, thanks to the idealization of

---

[1] " Now when proceeding along my path I reached the
new high road, I noticed a waggon, made of firm planks,
drawn by two oxen, the largest and strongest of foreign
breed.   Beside them a maiden walked with firm tread,
with a long staff she guided the two powerful animals,
now urging them on, now holding them back, she led them
wisely."

things seen with the eye, carry us " into quite strange regions," as Humboldt expresses it, or rather, as we express it, into the regions of beautiful literature (here " beauty " and " ideality " are equivalent in meaning to literature) ; and we not only happen to forget (this also is Humboldt's remark) that " the long staff which serves as a goad and a guide is no longer customary with us," but we forget a great many other things, which are perhaps of greater consequence.

We too admire, for they are truly admirable, the impulses of feeling ; for instance, the earnest entreaties of the mother who would induce her son to confide in her :

Mutter, sagt er betroffen, ihr überrascht mich ! Und eilig
Trocknet er ab die Thränen, der Jüngling edlen Gefühles.
Wie ? du weinest, mein Sohn ? versetzte die Mutter
  betroffen ;
Darum kenn' ich dich nicht ! ich habe das niemals
  erfahren !
Sag' was beklemmt dir das Herz ? was treibt dich,
  einsam zu sitzen
Unter dem Birnbaum hier ? Was bringt dir Thränen ins
  Auge ? [1]

[1] " Mother—he said, astonished,—you surprise me ! And hastily he wiped away his tears, this youth of noble feeling,— What ? You are weeping, my son ?—answered his mother in astonishment. This is very unlike you ! It is the first time I have seen this ! Say, what is it that oppresses your heart ? What makes you sit here alone under the pear tree ? What brings tears to your eyes ? "

Or when Dorothea tells of her first husband, who left to fight for the cause of liberty and who perished in the massacres in France :

Als ihn die Lust, in neuern veränderten Wegen zu wirken,
Trieb, nach Paris zu gehen, dahin, wo er Kerker und
    Tod fand :
—Lebe glücklich, sagt' er. Ich gehe ; denn alles bewegt
    sich
Jetzt auf Erden einmal, es scheint sich alles zu trennen.
Grundgesetze lösen sich auf den festesten Staaten,
Und es löst der Besitz sich los vom alten Besitzer,
Freund sich los von Freund ; so löst sich Liebe von
    Liebe . . .
Also sprach er ; und nie erschien der Edle mir wieder.[1]

At the same time we cannot but notice that all this is stylized.

We admire the " epic fulness," the " calm epic narration," which the above-mentioned critics commend as some virtue which the genius of Goethe bestowed on German culture. The mother is seeking Hermann, does not find him in his usual spots, and says to herself that he is in the garden :

[1] " When the desire to develop his activity in modern and different spheres drove him to go to Paris, where he met with imprisonment and death :—Live in happiness, he said. I must go ; for now everything on earth seems to move at once, everything seems to be dissolved. Fundamental laws are disappearing in the most firmly constituted states and posessions are being torn from the hands of the ancient possessor. Friend leaves friend ; thus love must separate itself from love. . . . Thus he spake ; and I have never seen my noble lover since."

Da durchschritt sie behende die langen doppelten Höfe,
Liess die Ställe zurück und die wohlgezimmerten
  Scheunen,
Trat in den Garten, der weit bis an die Mauern des
  Städtchens
Reichte, schritt hindurch und freute sich jeglichen
  Wachstums,
Stellte die Stützen zurecht, auf denen beladen die Äste
Ruhten des Apfelbaums, wie des Birnbaums lastende
  Zweige,
Nahm gleich einige Raupen vom kräftig strotzenden
  Kohl weg ;
Denn ein geschäftiges Weib thut keine Schritte verge-
  bens.[1]

But we do not deceive ourselves with the belief that this fulness and attention to detail, this epithetizing are anything more than a rather happy jest.

There is a jesting tone, too, in the invocation to the Muses, which almost seems to belong to the mock-heroic, or to remind us of the *Giorno* of Parini :

Musen, die ihr so gern die herzliche Liebe begünstigt,
Auf dem Wege bisher den trefflichen Jüngling geleitet,
An die Brust ihm das Mädchen noch vor der Verlobung
  gedrückt habt :

[1] "Then quickly she hastened through the two long courtyards, past the stables and the well-built granaries, stepped into the garden, which reached to the walls of the little town, walked down the centre of the garden and rejoiced at the growth of every plant, fixed the stakes more firmly, on which rested heavy-laden the branches of the apple trees and the pear-trees, removed also some caterpillars from the sturdy cabbages ; for a busy woman takes no step in vain."

Helfet auch ferner den Bund des lieblichen Paares
vollenden,
Teilet die Wolken sogleich, die über ihr Glück sich
heraufziehn !
Aber saget vor allem, was jetzt im Hause geschiehet.[1]

In short, in *Hermann und Dorothea* we must not try to find Goethe at his greatest, although in this work doubtless a great poet amuses himself with the small and the minute and shows his greatness even in this self-amusement.

[1] " Muses, who gladly favour heartfelt love, who have hitherto accompanied on his path our excellent hero, have pressed to his heart his maiden even before the betrothal ; help to complete the bond of union of this loving pair, disperse forthwith the clouds which are gathering over their happiness ! But tell us first of all what is happening in the house."

XII

LYRICS

GOETHE'S lyrics are not, of course, as critics believe, who are still entangled in the mesh of rhetorical ideas, the "lyric poetry" of Goethe, since the latter coincides with his whole poetical work and even in its strongest and most powerful accents is to be found in the novels and dramas which we have already dealt with and in the other works which we shall mention. Neither are they his minor works, in the sense which this term sometimes assumes, of secondary works. On the contrary, as we know, they are to be placed among his most inspired and perfect compositions. So that "lyrics" and "minor works" they may be called solely for the purpose of a publisher's or a bookseller's classification, on account of their brevity, variety, and multiplicity, which induces one to collect them in separate series and subseries. In reality, however, they form one with the greater works, with which they are closely connected as anticipations, explanations and continuations.

We have already had occasion to allude to the lyrics of the "titanic" period, in writing which Goethe usually employed a metre which would now be termed free, a metre without external regularity and devoid of tradition and models, though he sometimes imagined in the case of a few of these lyrics that he had had Pindar and the Pindaric fury in mind, a Pindar, however, whom he followed unconsciously and from afar. These poems in free metre—apart from their singular force and beauty—are worthy of notice, because they show, in the first place, how free verse, which the spokesmen of modernism (cold intellectualists despite their disorderly measures) recommend and would wish to see adopted as the usual form, suitable for all mental states and for all petty emotions, was used by Goethe, who was a true and a great poet, only at one period of his life, very rarely, and for very special sources of inspiration. He was, moreover, very careful not to reduce it to a manner, and, just as he had used them formerly, so he again used, with

a master's hand, restrained traditional metres.
Since the lyrics of this series, in spite of their
apparent freedom, follow a rigid law in the
rhythm which is adopted, in the variations
which they undergo, in the inequalities which
resolve themselves in the total equality, in
the proportion of the parts, they show, in
the second place, that the poet did not have
recourse to such a form (as contemporary
poets usually do) for the sake of convenience
or from laziness, or because it is excessively
easy to use, but in obedience to an inner
necessity and to an exquisite feeling for art.
Any one of these lyrics will serve to prove this,
for example, one which is as short as it is
admirable, *An Schwager Kronos*, composed
on a journey, when Goethe was driving
through hilly country in a heavy mail-coach,
now rapidly descending, now ascending slowly
and wearily. Whereupon, in the feeling and
the fancy of this dreaming traveller poet,
the driver is changed into Kronos, the god
of Time, the journey becomes that of life, the
quick descent becomes youth's race towards
the tumult of the world, the wearisome
ascent becomes the struggles that human
work demands, the prospect, which opens
out on the height, becomes the pleasures of

art and meditation, the refreshing draught, offered by the maiden on the threshold, becomes love and pleasure. Then suddenly again the descent towards the setting sun, towards his destination, symbolizes the journey towards death, towards a death desired without old age and decay, in full fervour and zest, which makes one willingly accept and undertake the leap into the dark abyss, the journey to Orcus, not reluctantly, with no repugnance, since, although it is the last act, it is an act of life, a necessary stage, the end, but at the same time the fulfilment of living, without which the preceding acts would have neither meaning nor beginning. Here poetry does not need rhyme or regular verses to enclose the emotion in a perfect circle.

Just as the feeling for rhythm and for rhythmical unity is very strong in these free lyrics, so the colour of the images (we mention these as two distinct things, whereas they are in reality one) never offends us by shrill-ness, accumulation or exaggeration, which are the favourite sins of the Romanticists and, worse still, of the Impressionists and Deca-dents of to-day, who are all out of harmony, out of sympathy, out of tune. The sober, terse and realistic details do not remain material, they assume an inner, sentimental value, and, at the same time, with their fresh decisiveness they prevent the feeling from expressing itself confusedly and losing itself in indefiniteness. The pervading quality of this sublime and truly æsthetic calm does not lack playful touches, such as, to keep to the lyric which we have taken as an example, the figure of Orcus, who, on hearing the sound of the postillion arriving and the pawing of the horses, comes forward to welcome the new arrivals. He comes forward like a host (*Wirth*) with the friendly (*freundlich*), professional smile with which a host greets his customers.

The same calm, which here and there permits a slightly ironical tone, forms one of the charms of Goethe's ballads, a species of compositions which with Schiller became subtle, artificial, anecdotical tales, without an inner poetical motive, and with the Romanticists endeavoured to introduce the mysterious, the terrible, the extravagant, the astonishing that impresses the multitude, merely babbled in the impossible effort, and finally called forth the parodies which they deserved. But Goethe treated some of these popular fancies and legendary tales in open fun, with good-natured roguishness (as *Wirkung in die Ferne* or *Ritter Kurts Brautfahrt*); others with a gnomic or a satirical purpose (as the *Schatzgräber*, the *Wandelnde Glocke*, the *Zauberlehrling*); and even those in which he felt the attraction of the dread and the mysterious (as the *Fischer* or the *Erlkönig*) he treated musically, refining and spiritualizing the material element in order to make it imply something deeply and universally human. Even where he is seized by an ethical emotion, such as the redemption of the courtesan by the power of love, as in *Der Gott und die Bajadere*, one notices that he tries, nevertheless, to avoid the solemness, the anguish, and the torture, and not to enter too much into the problem of passion. Therefore he tells the story partly seriously, partly lightly, as can be noticed in the almost comical bit of dialogue in the first meeting between the inexperienced god and the bayadera :

> Grüss dich, Jungfrau !—Dank der Ehre !
> Wart, ich komme gleich hinaus. . . .

and also at the end, which seems the *fabula docet* of a beast fable, this purpose of Goethe can be felt, especially in the metre and the

rhythm which he uses, a purpose achieved
without disturbing the humanity, the tenderness which yet transpires from the tale,
which is so lightly and merrily versified.
Even where the accent is tragic, where Goethe
strikes one of the deepest chords of his
naturalistic and anti-ascetic belief, in the
Braut von Korinth (which is the queen
of all these ballads), the tragic element
rises gradually from a tranquil and detailed
narrative, which finally ends in an outburst
of despair and indignation. Herder, who
fostered the taste for pseudopopular romantic
ballads, found and must have found these
masterpieces of Goethe frivolous and lacking
in morality.

In his love songs Goethe usually adopted,
on the one hand, popular models, i.e. simple
elementary songs which the people fashion
or love to repeat and to appropriate, and, on
the other hand, especially in the poems of
his earlier years, the erotic, melodious ditties
of the eighteenth century, somewhat pastoral
and arcadian. Love songs they are, but they
do not sing of the *pathos* of love, such as one
finds in the love songs of other poets and in
the novels and tragedies of Goethe himself,
but rather of love such as he was wont to

feel it, as an emotion which he experienced with joy, with delight, not without trembling and palpitation and pangs, but in reality holding himself above it. One might call it in Goethe's case not love-passion but the game of love. Hence those popular forms and the light society verse, which had been used already to a certain extent to express the game of love, and had become almost a game themselves, came naturally to him. Even in these *Lieder* (which is the name under which they have become famous) Goethe overcomes entirely all that was trite and conventional in the erotic poetry of his time and all that is insipid in the imitation of popular songs. For he always chooses the rhythmical movements from an emotion which he has experienced, from some impulses which he has detected in his own heart, and he thus bestows on these small compositions grace, delicacy, and sweetness. Life and literature are completely fused in them, not because life passes over into literature, but because literature comes to life again, or rather yields to life. Even in his earliest poems, where the taste of the time prevails in certain epigrammatical endings, what skies and fields, and dawns, and nights, and moonlights, and breath of zephyrs! One of the earliest, *Die schöne Nacht*, closes with the charming thought that he would willingly give a thousand such beautiful nights for one which his beloved would give him. But the chief beauty is not this desire, is not the enjoyment of his beloved, but the enjoyment of the beautiful night itself:

> Wandle mit verhülltem Schritte
> Durch den öden finstern Wald:
> Luna bricht durch Busch und Eichen,
> Zephyr meldet ihren Lauf,
> Und die Birken streun mit Neigen
> Ihr den süssten Weihrauch auf. . . .[1]

The same may be said of the other *Lied*, where the moon appears with her lover, Endymion; yet, before being translated into the fashionable mythology of the time, the moon is here just the moon, seen by an impressionable soul, by a tender heart:

> Schwester von dem ersten Licht,
> Bild der Zärtlichkeit in Trauer!
> Nebel schwimmt mit Silberschauer
> Um dein reizendes Gesicht.[2]

---

[1] " . . . wander with silent steps through the dark, deserted forest; Luna breaks through bushes and oak-trees, Zephyr heralds her course, and the birches bowing offer her sweet incense."

[2] " Sister of the first light, tenderness clothed in mourning! A quivering silvery mist floats round thy dear countenance."

The few poems to Lida form a contrast
to these love poems, which are emotional,
pleasant, trembling, caressing in spirit, but
not powerfully affecting. This difference
was noticed by the poet himself, when, during
his last years, he expressed pleasure that a
critic should have noticed that in the former
" there was more tenderness than in all the
others." Whether they were composed or
not for Frau von Stein, or whether they do
or do not allude to the reality and the peculiar
circumstances of that love (which is of little
or no consequence to us), lyrics such as
Warum gabst du uns . . . or *Der Becher* or
the poem entitled *An Lida* have a singularly
impassioned accent, which nevertheless does
not disturb even here the harmony of the
form, nor sully its purity. The first of these
voices in a manner both deep and delicate
the torture of love in intellectual and refined
beings, who discern and wish to discern and
understand each the feeling of the other.
Der Becher, song of joy, of gratitude, of
religious worship for the woman admired,
who finally yields to her lover who has long
desired her, is like an artistic goblet which
the poet chisels for her and offers her, with
scenes of pagan deities, which serve as a

foundation for the triumph of this woman and this love. *An Lida* extols her image, which always accompanies him in the tumult of life, likening it to the eternal stars, which shine constant through the variable light of the aurora borealis. In these poems, as in all the poems of this small series, the expression is more immediate and direct, without the complacency and the delicate coquetting and toying with literary form, of which there is a trace in the *Lieder*.

Goethe returned, however, to a similar complacency in the *Römische Elegien*, for which, what was elsewhere supplied to him by pastoral and popular poetry, was offered to him by the poetry of the " triumviri " (Catullus, Tibullus, and Propertius) and of the other Latin erotic poets ; and here, too, in the most spontaneous fashion, by the very quality of the love which he sings of, by the pictures of Rome and of his Roman sojourn, which filled his imagination, and which, forming a background for his love, gave it an appearance at once exotic and ancient, and let him enjoy it with a particular sense of voluptuousness. The metre and the Latin movements have in the *Römische Elegien* (as in other elegies and epistles and in the epigrams) a much closer connection with the subject than in *Hermann und Dorothea*. So that the *Elegien* should not properly be reckoned as humanistic poetry ; at most they resemble the hendecasyllabic *Baiae* and the other songs of Pontano, who in a rather similar fashion combined his ardent voluptuousness, his capacity for enjoyment with the voluptuousness of ancient forms, with the enjoyment of the measures of the Roman love poets.

Froh empfind' ich mich nun auf klassischem Boden begeistert,
Vor- und Mitwelt spricht lauter und reizender mir . . .
Amor schüret die Lamp' indess und denket der Zeiten,
Da er den nämlichen Dienst seinen Triumvirn gethan.[1]

The theme of the *Römische Elegien* is the physical joy of love, of physical love, which in the calm of satisfied senses contemplates the world with gladness, human creatures with indulgence and sympathy and first among them the beloved woman from whom he demands neither the spirituality of kinship of soul, nor virtues to admire and revere, but the freshness of youth, beauty in its

[1] " I feel myself filled with joy on classic soil, past and present speak to me more clearly and more sweetly. . . . Meanwhile Amor blows the lamp into flame and thinks of the times when he performed the same service for his triumvirs."

splendour and joyous health, and that con-
descending and playful chatter that one can
have with children. Sometimes he even
poetises in her arms, as she sleeps, as he feels
her close to him like some splendid animal :

Oftmals hab' ich auch schon in ihren Armen gedichtet
Und des Hexameters Mass leise mit fingernder Hand
Ihr auf den Rücken gezählt. Sie atmet in lieblichem
  Schlummer,
Und es durchglühet ihr Hauch mir bis ins Tiefste die
  Brust.[1]

This kind of poetry, in order to merit the
name of poetry, must preserve a kind of
immodesty, unconscious of being immodest,
innocent, the peculiar quality of him who
in such moments neither sees nor feels anything else in the world but his closed circle
of happiness. In this Goethe succeeds extra-
ordinarily well.

The maxims of wisdom which appear in
some *Lieder* and in some ballads, occupy the
first place in another large number of Goethe's
lyrics, in the lyrics which we might call
"didactic," eliminating from this word all
trace of censure and removing from it the
æsthetic contradiction which it seems to

---

[1] " Often have I poetised in her arms and with fingering
hand have gently counted out the hexameter's measure on
her back. She breathes in sweet slumber, and her breath
penetrates deep down into my breast."

contain. There is, it is true, a species of didactic lyric or poetry which is contradictory and repugnant; for when the mind has raised itself by means of reflexion, speculation and criticism to grasp a truth in its ideal and systematic relations, it forces itself in vain to express this truth again in a confused and fanciful form, which is henceforth unsuited to it. Hence the dualism of the symbol and the concept symbolized, of the thought and the form, metrical or otherwise determined, attached to it from outside. This does not mean to say that this truth, if worked out critically, does not proceed in its own way from vital emotions, since, if it were not so, it would be merely cold pedantry and servile scholasticism; but from the emotional incident the spirit has then raised itself to the other emotion and passion of contemplating the real and the true for their own sake; and this demands its peculiar expression, its peculiar lyric, such as one finds in the concretely abstract pages of the great philosophers, which are so poetical in their severe prose. The would-be philosophers and would-be poets, on the other hand, combining two weaknesses, compose symbolical and didactic poetry, *sensu deteriori*.

But if, instead of a mind which rises to speculation, criticism and system, one thinks of the case of a mind in firm possession of ideas and convictions, which reacts in contemplation of the varied spectacle of human passions, promptly re-establishing the balance that the latter seems to disturb, and reproduces this emotion, illuminating it at the same time with the interpretation of reason, one can easily understand how a didactic composition can be produced which has nevertheless lyrical value, namely, a reflection which unites with beauty. Such was the case with Goethe, and this is what he meant when he said (however exact or inexact the formula may sound) that his thinking was "intuitive." Hence his didactic lyrics are lively and stirred, outlined and coloured. Proofs of this are the hymns *Das Göttliche*, *Grenzen der Menschheit*, *Meine Göttin*, the *Episteln*, the *Epigramme*, those *Antiker Form sich nähernd*, those of the *Vier Jahreszeiten*, the *Xenien* and the *Zahme Xenien*, and very many other poems and shorter poems, gnomic or satirical. Further, the philosophical lyrics (belonging to the cycle *Gott und Welt*) offer some conclusions from philosophy which more immediately stir the soul and more closely concern practical conduct and life.

The last great lyrical harvest which Goethe reaped was the *Divan*, in which didactic or hortatory poetry is reintroduced as well as the graceful poetry of love (in the book of Suleika), both no longer clinging to national popular or Græco-Roman forms, but clothed in Oriental garb, in accordance with another historical and literary interest, which had taken shape at that time in the mind of Europe, and which the productive and versatile Goethe this time, too, not so much accepted and followed, as he himself created and furthered. But his last profound lyrical cry is the *Elegie*, entitled *Marienbader Elegie*, composed at the age of seventy-four— the hopeless reblossoming of love in the heart of an old man—to which he added the following year a significant preface addressed to the form of Werther, to the "much lamented shade," which did not fear to appear before him, like some ever-threatening Fate.

XIII

THE *WAHLVERWANDTSCHAFTEN*

ON account of the fact that Goethe rapidly passed through various spiritual phases, enriched by an active mental life of research and meditation, it is not possible to treat his works, as is rightly done in the case of other artists, as a series developing from a single fundamental motive which passes through various degrees or which appears now under one, now under another aspect. Even as regards the period of his maturity one can generally say only what has been said already, i.e., that he preserved himself in a condition of robust wisdom, a wisdom which, however, dominates little by little new mental states, varying with that powerful and manifold vitality.

For about the year 1807 his mind was gripped (owing to circumstances which do not interest us and upon which we shall let biographers enlarge, who are frequently as

indiscreet and vulgar as they are fantastic in
their conjectures) by the feeling of the
devastating power of passionate love, no
longer viewed as overthrowing and dragging
along with it every obstacle in its mad onrush,
but as contrasted with a resisting force,
spiritually higher, i.e. the ethical institution
of marriage. A feeling of dissension and
struggle, which was termed later the problem
of the "right of love," called forth innumerable problem novels and problem plays, left
its mark on legislation and, taken up by
coarse democratic minds, which reason in an
empty manner, assumes the form of admirable
solutions which, if put into practice, would
very probably bring society back to that
"bestial state," of which Vico speaks, from
which it raised itself, thanks to weddings,
tribunals, and altars. Goethe, who was a
man of heart and serious intellect, did not
side sentimentally with love against marriage,
as many Romanticists did. But he could
not at all consider that the contest was such
that it could be fought out in a formal manner
with chivalrous weapons and end quickly
with the easy victory of the worthier com-
batant. He felt it rather as a terrible and pro-
foundly human struggle, which not even the

choicest souls can be certain of being spared; and, if they sin against the moral law, the victory of the latter is ruthless, involving the sacrifice, the unhappiness and the death of the individual. And since the moral law is a universal law, placed in the centre of the world that it controls and governs, its manifestation in this struggle appeared to him to be what the believer terms the " hand of God," and others " chance," but what the poet considers is but the symbol of the power of this law, which bends and turns the course of events to its own purpose.

Charlotte and Eduard are the married couple whom Goethe introduces to us as peaceful and happy in the quiet of the country. Youthful lovers, separated by fortune, they have recently married, when Charlotte became a widow. But, of the two, the woman has the greater foresight; she knows or feels that virtue, however excellent and solid it may be, must be helped by prudence or, as the Evangelist says, whoever loves danger perishes therein. Hence, against the advice of her husband, she hesitates to invite to their house her young niece, Ottilie, and her husband's friend, the Captain. But Eduard's will prevails, the guests arrive and immediately love, that insidious and destructive passion, appears and begins its work. Eduard immediately falls in love with Ottilie. The morning after her arrival he says to his wife with great enthusiasm : " She is a very pleasant, entertaining girl." " Entertaining ? " retorts Charlotte with a smile. " Why, she hasn't yet opened her mouth ! " " Really ? " Eduard replies, trying to recollect, " that's very strange ! " Gradually Eduard and Ottilie meet, seek one another, confide in one another, amuse one another, share one another's interests, and become bound by common likes and dislikes, whilst, on the other hand, something similar takes place between Charlotte and the Captain ; and between the two new couples who are thus being formed there is even a tone of slight, veiled, unconscious hostility.

Goethe compares what follows in these cases with the chemical process, which brings together the combination of two substances with that of two others, thus producing a new double combination, in which one of the two first substances unites with one of the two second and the other with the remaining one. Hence the title of the novel : " elective affinities." It was against this

comparison and the thought that it suggests
that early censors rose up, accusing the
poet of materialism, mechanism and immoral
fatalism. Whereas it is just this, that in love
attractions arise apart from any deliberation
or will and, viewed from the moral observatory, appear to be extraneous, adverse forces,
and hence natural and mechanical, just as
Goethe considers them to be, not, therefore,
in opposition to morality, but rather in
conformity with the logic of the latter.

The severance and recombination of the
two couples proceeds irresistibly and speedily ;
their bodies remain pure, but their hearts
soon become entirely diverted from their
first directions and turn in different directions.
Eduard loves Ottilie, Charlotte loves the
Captain ; and, intoxicated by their love, one
night Eduard enters Charlotte's room and
they embrace one another madly, thus com-
mitting a double spiritual adultery. And
when at daybreak " Eduard awoke on the
breast of his wife, it seemed to him that the
day was dawning full of foreboding, that the
sun was shedding its light on a crime ; he
crept away gently from her side and, strange
to say, she found herself alone when she
awoke." At table both eye Ottilie and the

Captain furtively, with a feeling of shame and repentance, "for love is of that nature that it believes that it alone has rights and all other rights disappear before it."

The situation becomes such that it proves to be intolerable. Charlotte and the Captain, having exchanged their first kiss and felt the abyss beneath them, have had the strength of mind to leave one another and to resist the attraction which drives them together. But Ottilie is indeed devoured by passion and jealously and proudly shuts her heart to her friend and relative. Eduard thinks that he can never and under no condition renounce her. All that he is able to do is to go away for a time, return to the army which he had formerly belonged to, and expose himself to the dangers of war, as if to seek there the judgment of God. What he accepts, therefore, is nothing but a temporary absence. But the very safety in which he comes out of danger brings him back more resolutely to the passion which Ottilie, for her part, has preserved intact and cherished jealously in her silent heart. Meanwhile Charlotte has given birth to a son, the child of the double adultery, her own and Eduard's child, who has the large eyes of Ottilie and whose face bears traces of the features of the Captain. Eduard had spoken clearly to his wife: they had made a great mistake in attempting to revive at a certain age the desires and hopes of youth, forgetting that man experiences a complete change every ten years and that therefore one must ever look forward and never backward. So now he tells the Captain that he is willing to divorce Charlotte, and suggests a new double marriage. But when Ottilie sees Eduard again out of doors in the country, whilst she is carrying in her arms the child which has been entrusted to her, on her return crossing the lake in a boat, the child escapes from her arms and is drowned.

The death of this child which should never have been born, this death of which Ottilie has been the unwilling cause, marks the catastrophe. For although Charlotte now withdraws her refusal and is ready to consent to a divorce and a fresh marriage, Ottilie recovers from the blindness of her passion and decides that she can never and ought never to call Eduard hers, and that happiness is not to be her lot since she has not been worthy of it. She has left its path, has broken its law, she has even lost consciousness of it (as she says herself), and a hostile demon, who has now taken possession of her, prevents her from regaining her inner harmony. She runs away, therefore, to give herself up to the duties of governess and teacher, which are best carried out by those who have suffered greatly and have renounced the joy of living. But she is found again and brought back to her home ; and here, in the company of Eduard and Charlotte, she moves about dumb, in a self-imposed silence, so that Eduard feels that she is now far from him, that she has, as it were, raised herself above him. And preserving her vow of silence, she allows herself to die from abstinence. Eduard, whom she has forced to live, does not dare to disobey her, but the effort costs him great sacrifice, resignation is impossible and, consuming himself in this torment, he, too, dies soon after. Charlotte and the Captain continue to live separated.

This is a dramatic incident which takes place among people of noble and pure feelings, cultured, refined, and reflective minds, and who, therefore, play, one might say, with open cards, face to face with their own passions, never allowing their imagination to deceive them save in a few crises which

they themselves recognize subsequently as
such, scarcely ever building up fallacious
arguments for themselves, excellent reasoners,
who discuss among themselves the disease
which has attacked them in various forms.
The other characters, too, have the same
characteristics. Among them the same
dramatic incident is represented in another
fashion or is reflected, as, for instance, the
Baron and the Baroness, both married and
illegal lovers, and excellent Mittler, a specialist
on the subject of matrimonial discords, who
vainly endeavour to restore the various
differences to their former harmony. The
same characteristic, that of reflectiveness and
reasoning, is noticeable, too, in the episodical
and minor characters, such as the Assistant
at the school where Ottilie has been brought
up, and the young Architect. Pyschological
remarks and wise moral sayings are ever on
the lips of all these characters and, since
passion does not deaden their habitual
activity and their refined mental occupations,
a large portion of the book is devoted to
descriptions of the work of embellishment
which Eduard and his friends are carrying
out in the country where they live, and to
discussions on art ; and there are even

inserted fragments of a diary of Ottilie, which contains Goethe's thoughts on the most diverse subjects. Looking at it from the outside, one might even say that the passion theme is merely a pretext for something else ; but looking at it from within, one notices how this enlarging on various extraneous subjects is facilitated by the style of this work of art, which rather gains by this somewhat heavy, let us say, German framework. In spite of this large intellectual element, which characterizes the author and with which he imbues his characters and stamps their lives, the story develops powerfully. The characters, despite their general common physiognomy, which we have already described, are individualized. Eduard with his inability to deny himself a pleasure, his highest aspiration being what he calls happiness, in spite of this, never rough or coarse, perpetually young and also something of a child ; for instance, when he hears from Ottilie that his friend the Captain does not admire his musical talent, he is seized with fury and, nevertheless, " feels himself freed from all obligations to him " ; and lastly, after the death of Ottilie and the promise he has made her, he confesses to himself that " one

requires genius even for martyrdom " ;
Ottilie who, in the strange situation in which
she enters and remains with regard to
Charlotte, never rebels or refuses to carry out
her formal duty and is one of those natures
which are as thorough in erring as they are
heroic in making amends ; Charlotte, prudence personified, who has yet flesh, blood
and nerves ; the Captain, who can master
himself like a man. And although in the
last pages, in the narrative of the death and
of the transfiguration, as it were, of Ottilie
into a martyr and saint, the style becomes
perhaps slightly sentimental and affected, in
the remainder of the work the reader is
continually struck by the miracle of the
combination of the delicate with the simple,
never disturbed but merely varied or sometimes interrupted by the wealth of ethical
thoughts and psychological remarks.

XIV

THE *WANDERJAHRE*

THE *Wahlverwandtschaften* was the last dramatic creation which Goethe really lived through and transmuted into poetry. In *Wilhelm Meisters Wanderjahre* (from which the *Wahlverwandtschaften* was detached and dealt with separately as it deserved to be) the dramatic element is beginning to fail, or rather it is still kindled once more, but is suppressed and choked before it can burst into flame and burn like fire. The general dramatic situation, which in the *Wahlverwandtschaften* was encircled by a framework which was perhaps rather heavy, becomes itself in the *Wanderjahre* the framework or, if one prefers it, the pretext; and, moreover, almost all the other dramatic elements, which are to be found in it, become part of the framework, or rather seem to be merely the means of making the story move forward. The strange wanderings of this

abstract character, devoid of personal con-
sistency, whom we met as Wilhelm Meister
in the *Lehrjahre*, and who now becomes in
reality an empty name, is, considered from
the point of view of art, without motive and
accidental. But the same cannot be said of
other figures and situations. Lenardo, who
has been supplicated by a child in the most
piteous manner to save her father and herself
and who has determined in his heart, although
he has not promised or pledged himself to
this effect, to do as much as he can for her,
and who has not succeeded in his intentions,
and, perhaps, has not done as much as he
ought to have done, and remains with
the uncertain remorse of having caused
by his deeds and his omissions the ruin of
this little family and this child, is a character
and a situation which is highly poetical.
" The form of this child (he says when
confiding to Wilhelm) always comes to my
mind again with the forms of my own people,
and my greatest fear is that I shall hear that
she has perished in the misfortune into which
I drove her : for my omission seemed to be
an act which would contribute to her ruin,
an increasing of her sad fate. A thousand
times already I have said to myself that this

feeling is at bottom only a weakness, that it
was only from fear of remorse, not from a
nobler feeling, that I had early adopted the
rule of never giving a promise. And now the
remorse, which I have fled from, seems to
be revenging itself on me by choosing this
case instead of a thousand others, in order to
torment me. At the same time, the image,
the form, which tortures me, is so pleasant,
so lovable, that I love to linger over it. And
when I think of it, the kiss which she pressed
on my hand seems to burn me still." Poetical
too is his anxious search for this being who
has disappeared, whom he has lost sight of,
in order to assure himself that kindly Providence has made amends for his error or to
make amends for it himself if it is necessary
and if it is still possible for him to do so.
Into this remorse, this human compassion,
this sense of justice, there has penetrated an
interest which is love, one of the many ways
in which man forms ideal images and in
which love is born. But the search for the
poor " nut-brown maiden " serves later as a
pretext for joining together the various parts
of the book, which refuse to be connected :
and this passionate search, which is used as
a mere expedient, becomes now and then

rather pedantic and puerile and even assumes an unconsciously comical touch. Another example. The tale of the " *Mann von fünfzig Jahren* " is also a development of the theme of " elective affinities." We are introduced to a father who is loved by a young girl and betrothed to her, and to a son in love with a widow to whom he desires to be betrothed ; two couples who, having entered into relations with one another, produce fresh combinations, that of the two young people and that of the man of fifty years with the lively and witty little widow ; a kind of *Wahlverwandtschaften* which tends to comedy and to a happy solution, as this time there are no ethical obstacles to the two new combinations, they are rather deserving of strong ethical approval. But the author does not seem to take sufficient interest in the tale, he does not maintain the same level. Consequently having reached a certain point the four characters cease to be the figures in the picture and become merely decorative factors in the general framework. This framework encloses a little of everything : psychological and moral observations, social and educational Utopias, short stories, tales and facetious sayings, all with the pretence of offering a great spiritual drama, a " comedy of the soul " and a " comedy of human society " (" comedy " taken in the mediæval Dantesque sense).

Of the several " intellectualisms of composition " which appear in the works of Goethe, none is as palpable and as striking as that of the *Wanderjahre*, in a manner too that is far from comprehensible. For it is not easy to understand the psychological process by which the author was led to it, and allowed himself to advance so far therein, and how he was able to justify his action to himself. The excuses which he made to others are of the usual kind, such as we already know, namely, that if this work was not " *aus einem Stück*," it was, on the other hand, " *in einem Sinne*," that " in this book, as in life, there are the necessary and the accidental, the determined and the irresolute, sometimes success and sometimes failure, whence there results a kind of infinity, which cannot be grasped and expressed in logical and rational words." These are nothing but the jests of a great man. Lewes, an English biographer and early critic of Goethe, said, with reference to this work, that an English writer would never have ventured to mystify the public in this fashion (we know that, among other things, Goethe, seeing that the volumes did not turn out to be the same size in print, ordered his secretary, Eckermann, to take material from some collections of his notes and opinions and to put them together under the title : *Aus dem Archiv der Makarie*, Makarie being one of the characters !) ; and, although German critics have not failed to protest against these words of Lewes, doubly irreverent towards Goethe and towards his German readers, I do not think the criticism of Lewes is false even as regards the latter. For, particularly in Goethe's time, there was in the mental attitude of German readers something which probably encouraged the author to yield to his syncretistic tendency and to indulge his weaknesses. It was the period of formless, confused literature, of the novels of Jean Paul and his imitators, of the " Humoristen " to whom Wilhelm alludes playfully in one of his letters to Natalie (Book 2, chapter 11): "If after this detailed narrative I have to confess that I have not yet reached the goal which I have set myself, and that I may only hope to reach it by a circuitous path, what shall I say ! How can I excuse myself ! At any rate I could

make the following excuse : If the humourist
is allowed to turn everything upside down,
if he boldly lets his reader extract from it,
understanding it only in part, what is to be
found in it, shall an intelligent, a sensible
man not be allowed to work in several
different directions in a seemingly eccentric
manner, so that one shall find them at length
reflected and collected in a single focus, and
learn to see how the most diverse influences
surrounding a man can drive him to a
decision, which he could not have taken in
any other way, either from an inner impulse
or from some external cause ? "

Nevertheless, the *Wanderjahre* are a
collection of pages which have come from
the mind of Goethe ; and although we do
not wish to exaggerate, as has frequently
been done, the importance of his pedagogical
Utopia and of his other social or socialistic
Utopias (which are very limited and of slight
value speculatively and still more so practi-
cally on account of the fact that they are
Utopias), we cannot sufficiently admire the
treasures of discernment and wisdom which
are poured out in abundance in this work.
On almost every page we have occasion to
admire. Here, for example, is one of the

many moral observations on the relations between man and woman : " The enthusiasm that one feels for a woman should never be confided to another woman ; they know one another too well to esteem one another worthy of such exclusive admiration. Men seem to them like buyers in a shop, where the merchant with his goods which he knows has the advantage, and can seize the opportunity of exhibiting them in the best light ; whereas the buyer steps in with a kind of innocence, he needs the article, he wants and desires it, and he is seldom in a position to consider it with the eye of a connoisseur. The former knows very well what he is selling, the latter does not always know what he is getting. But one cannot change this peculiarity in human life and intercourse, and it is as praiseworthy as it is necessary, for all desiring and wooing, all buying and exchanging is based on it." And who has ever, when speaking of the Jews, expressed better the efficacy of the Bible, that collection of sacred books, " which fit together so happily that from the most heterogeneous elements we gain the illusion of a whole : they are sufficiently complete to satisfy, sufficiently fragmentary to incite, sufficiently barbarous to challenge, sufficiently delicate to calm . . . " ? (Book 2, chapter 2). And, concerning the same subject, who has ever before, or better, or more concisely touched the essential point of all the real difficulties regarding the position of the Jews in modern society, when, in excluding them from his ideal republic (Book 3, chapter 11), Goethe remarked that one could not " grant them a share in the highest culture, of which they deny the origin and the tradition " ?

Even from an artistic point of view, if the great work of art, which the general plan seemed to aim at, is not realized, one discovers, nevertheless, everywhere in it *membra disiecta poetae*, as in the tale we have already mentioned of the " nut-brown " maiden, in the idyll with which the book opens, *Sanct Joseph der Zweite*, in the delightful tales *Wer ist der Verräter ?* and *Die neue Melusine*, in the female figures, as, for example, Hersilie, and also in the character which he conceived poetically, although he afterwards spoiled it in execution, old Makarie. All the pages contain a wealth of the most delicate turns, of which we shall give two short examples. The wild brother of wise Lucinde says : " On Saturdays Lucinde is of no use at all, for she brings father punctually the household accounts ; this is a business which I should have taken my share of, but God forbid ! If I know what a thing costs, I have no appetite for anything." The youth who has allowed himself to be reduced by magic to diminutive proportions in order to live in the kingdom of diminutive beings, tells the diminutive fairy Melusina : " Nevertheless I had not forgotten, unfortunately, my former condition. I detected within myself a standard of former greatness, which made me restless and unhappy. Now I grasped for the first time what the philosophers mean by their ideals, with which men are said to be so tormented. I had an ideal of myself and sometimes in a dream I appeared to myself as a giant."

XV

FAUST II

*F*AUST II certainly suffers from being joined to *Faust I* as a second part, appearing to form one work. The poetical reader, failing to find the true, inner continuation which he has been promised, and feeling himself in a world entirely different and almost opposite, cannot but feel disappointed and inclined to cast it aside in a spirit of condemnation. Hence the bitter opponents whom *Faust II* has met with, especially in Germany itself, who have now and then gone the length of openly contemning, deriding and even parodying it.

In order to do it the justice it deserves, one must consider it as it is, a work apart, and judge it by itself, not in relation to and by the standard of the other work from which, moreover, it is separated by an interval of

more than half a century, *grande aevi spatium*,
particularly for a poet.

Goethe, who during his whole life had
cherished the thought of a dramatic treatment of the Faust legend, and, after having
put in order the fragments he had already
composed in his youth, by arranging them
to form a first part, had resumed and then
discontinued work on the second and last
part, for which he had notes and plans
accumulated among his papers, wished during
his last years before leaving the world to
work out in some manner his plan, like a
painter who, having left untouched the
border of a wall, all of which has been painted
in the fire of inspiration, feels offended by
the sight of this empty space and resolves to
fill in the blank, though with a very different
eye and hand, merely to get rid of the feeling
of incompleteness and imperfection.

Thirty years ago he had not succeeded in
regaining the inspiration of an earlier period,
and still less was he going to succeed now,
after all that had happened in the meantime
around him and within himself. So he set
about his new work with the ideas and the
moral attitude which had since become
firmly fixed in his mind and had calmly taken

possession of his seventy-five years. We must look at Goethe as he was at that age, we must not let our glance wander or revert to the Goethe who composed Faust's soliloquy in his study or the tragedy of Gretchen.

The general form, which offered itself spontaneously for this new dramatization, was that of the " operatic libretto," a form in which Goethe had had considerable practice, for we must remember that among other things he was also one of the last Court poets, the Metastasio, as it were, of the little court at Weimar, for which he wrote many *Singspiele*, prologues, allegories and *Festlieder*. Since the " libretto " is not an independent poetical work, but rather the foundation of a work which music is to complete, it does not demand, rather it excludes, violent passion and solid poetry (so much so that in taking librettos from real dramas one abridges here and amplifies there, but one always renders them superficial). Therefore the new *Faust*, begun on this note, excluded what Goethe could no longer give, and welcomed with open arms what, on the other hand, he could still give and, one might even add, could only then give fully.

What was this ? The play of imagination

of an old artist, henceforth master of innumerable figures and situations drawn from reality
and from literature, who is glad to make them
pass through his mind again, toying with
them; and the wisdom of the man, experienced
in the world and human thought, who has
already witnessed so many mental and moral
vicissitudes, and without for this reason
becoming sceptical or callous, has rather
saved for himself a strong faith of his own.
He is no longer roused to excessive enthusiasm
or to violent contempt. His wisdom is often
softened by a smile. Even his faith he
expresses discreetly, sometimes borrowing a
jesting tone.

That such are the contents and the corresponding form of *Faust II*—from the scene
in the Imperial Court, with the speeches of
the Chancellor, the Treasurer, the Marshal
and the War Minister, the appearance of
Mephistopheles as Court Fool and the suc-
ceeding Carnival, the calling up of Helena
before the Court as spectators, the distilling
of Homunculus, the classical Walpurgis-night,
the union of Helena with Faust, and so
forth, to the easy manner with which the
little angels snatch from Mephistopheles the
"immortal part of him," and to the assump-

tion of this immortal part, the soul of Faust,
into the Catholic Paradise—will be easily
noticed by any reader who reads Goethe
and the book without introducing extraneous
ideas.   And although he may happen to hit
on certain passages which seem to possess,
and do in reality possess, greater or diverse
intensity, as, for instance, the return of Helena
to the royal palace of Sparta, or the *terzine*
with which Faust greets the sunrise, he will
remember that the former was composed at
a much earlier stage in the development of
Goethe and was afterwards introduced into
Faust II, and that the *terzine*, according
to information supplied to us by Goethe's
biographers, were also, if not exactly written
down, conceived and drafted several decades
earlier.   In other passages, where great
drama or great lyric poetry are just
touched, the latter are suddenly dropped,
as one can notice, for instance, in the
moment of great expectation when the
journey of Faust to the mysterious Mothers
is announced : " Goddesses (says Mephistopheles), unknown to you mortals and
whom we name reluctantly."   " Thither
(says the same preceptor) there is no
road ! To where none have ever trod,

none will ever tread; a road to where none have ever prayed to go, nor ever will pray to go. Are you ready?—There are no locks there, no bolts. You will be surrounded by solitudes. . . . Finally a glowing tripod will indicate to you that you are at the very deepest bottom. By its light you will see the Mothers, some sitting, others standing and walking, as it may be. Formation, transformation, the Eternal play of the Eternal mind, surrounded by images of all creatures. They will not see you, for they can only see shadows." Faust decides to undertake the journey, full of courage, hoping "in your nothing to find the all." But the journey is neither represented nor described. We only hear about it in the partly grotesque, partly charlatan allusions of Mephistopheles. When Helen is called up before the Emperor and his Court, and knights and ladies make prosaic and gossiping remarks about her form and that of Paris, Faust, the conjuror. is seized with heroic passion for Beauty:

Hab' ich noch Augen? Zeigt sich tief im Sinn
Der Schönheit Quelle reichlichstens ergossen?
Mein Schreckensgang bringt seligsten Gewinn,
Wie war die Welt mir nichtig, unerschlossen!

.   .   .   .   .   .

Du bist's der ich die Regung aller Kraft,
Den Inbegriff der Leidenschaft,
Dir Neigung, Lieb', Anbetung, Wahnsinn zolle.[1]

Whereupon Mephistopheles, from the prompter's box, calms him, telling him to collect himself and " not forget his part : "

So fasst euch doch und fallt nicht aus der Rolle![2]

Faust, in truth, does not " forget his part " and, shortly afterwards, ends childishly by throwing himself on the spirit, seized with jealousy at seeing Paris kiss Helen. Thus it always happens, even in the scenes which are concerned with Faust's activity and redemption, worked out with the usual lightness of the libretto ; so that one can easily understand the remark of Theodor Vischer that " Faust has never really striven (*erstrebt*) and is redeemed (*erlöst*) very easily."

What has already been said proves how ineffectual are the efforts of those who examine closely and interpret every scene and every detail with the object of discovering therein

---

[1] " Have I yet eyes ? Deep within my heart does the fountain of beauty appear to me, flowing fully ? My journey of horror has its most blessed reward. How empty, undiscovered the world was to me ! . . . 'Tis thou, to whom I give the impulse of all my strength, the concentration of all my passion, inclination, love, adoration, madness."

[2] " Collect yourself and don't forget your part ! "

and making clear the plan and the unity of the work. Of course, there is a certain plan and a certain unity in *Faust II*, for such there must be in the composition of any work, but it is very extrinsic and general, and can be stated in a few words. Faust has an experience of public life at the Emperor's Court, and suddenly leaves it in order to follow the ideal of beauty and art (Helena), an ideal which vanishes, merging into that of a life of activity ; therefore he co-operates in helping the Emperor to win a battle, and receives from the latter in fee the sea-coast, where he accomplishes a great work of improvement, finding therein full satisfaction for his soul, and, by this means, he saves himself for Eternity, having conquered and put Mephistopheles to shame. But the elaboration of this simple plot is extremely varied and whimsical. The true artistic unity lies precisely in the half-jesting tone, the tone which prevails usually and more generally in the various parts.

Not less than the pedantic interpreters do those err who extol this last form of Goethe's poetry as a quintessential, superior poetry of the heights where the image becomes concept and the concept becomes image. When poetry becomes superior in this manner, that is to say, superior to itself, it loses rank as poetry and should be termed rather "inferior poetry," namely, wanting in poetry and rich in imagination and spirit. So that it is vain to seek in *Faust II* the poetical depth which is to be found, on the other hand, in the Easter scene or in Gretchen's madness in prison, that is to say, the very depth of art, which snatches and renders again a vital impulse, in which the infinite vibrates concretely, in which we therefore discover inexhaustible vistas, and which no concept can ever equal.

Neither must we think that there is, on the other hand, great philosophical depth in *Faust II*, since in its limited species it is and remains poetry, is not and does not become philosophy, and the ideas therein are not thought out or reasoned out. They are only more or less clearly referred to. Now an idea which is merely referred to and is not developed or followed up critically is a static idea, dead, vague, indeterminate. This fact explains the innumerable treatises of the commentators of Goethe, Dante, and all other poets who have composed allegories, since it is impossible to determine what in the poet himself, in creating the image, was not and could not be determined, even if, apart from the image, it had any determination in his mind. The only resource is for the poet to write a commentary on his own works and to state definitely what were his thoughts, such as we have in certain commentaries of Bruno and Campanella on their own works. In this case the depth is to be found in the commentary, not in the poetry on which the commentary is written, in the idea, the real idea, and not in the symbol. But Goethe not only did not write commentaries on his own works, but even, as we know, eluded the questions of his friends and disciples regarding the hidden meanings, the secrets which he had " stowed away " in the inventions of *Faust II* ; nor, on the other hand, was he temperamentally so cold as to conceive transparent allegories in the manner of a Martianus Capella or some mediæval author. With regard to this point one may admit that the allegories in *Faust*, rather than allegories, are often myths which Goethe fashioned with the ambiguity and multiplicity of meanings which is the peculiar quality of myths. What idea underlies the manufacture of paper money, guaranteed by the treasures hidden in the ground, which

Mephistopheles promotes in the Empire, showering happiness on all, from the Emperor to the meanest beggar? Perhaps a criticism of promissory notes? That would be foolish. Or the abuse of paper money circulation? That would not be original. And what idea underlies the marriage of Faust and Helena? Is it, as it has been stated to be, the union of the Teutonic spirit with that of Greece? That would be an historical error and, at most, a nationalistic boasting, foreign to Goethe's nature. Is it the invocation of the union of new inspiration with perfection of form, which is considered to be the characteristic of Greek art? That, too, would hardly be original and, lacking the critical process which justifies and determines it, would be open to several objections and misconceptions. And the symbolizing of George Byron in Euphorion, the son of Faust and Helena, has this any critical value for the understanding of Byron's poetry? An Italian reader would say that this symbol, if it suits any poet, would suit much better the restrained and classical poet of sorrow, Leopardi, or the singer of the *Sepolcri* and the *Grazie*, than the unbridled, disorderly, miry genius of Byron. All this is said not in censure of Goethe, who was free to imagine and devise and exaggerate and jest as he pleased, but in censure of those who read hidden meanings into his work and treat *Faust II* with a seriousness which this poem does not demand and which does not correspond to the manner in which it took shape in the mind of the poet.

After having gained some familiarity with *Faust II* by means of a first reading, which should partake of the nature of a study of the text, it is advisable, when re-reading it, not to read it from beginning to end, as one does in the case of *Werther* or the story of Gretchen, but to open it here and there, in order to witness a phantasmagoria, to enjoy a little picture, to smile at a satirical description, to pick out some fine saying. In the masquerade Goethe revives the carnival songs of the Italian Renascence ; and it would be an indication of very bad taste if we were to turn all our attention to the so-called " grand drama of humanity," of which Faust is supposed to be the representative, and to the significance of the masquerade in this drama, and were not to pause at each of these masques ; for example, at the little speech of the Punchinelloes, who describe their own ideal of life, or at the mother, who is worried about

her daughter, for whom she has not succeeded
in getting a husband :

> Mädchen, als du kamst an's Licht
> Schmückt ich dich im Häubchen,
> Warst so lieblich von Gesicht,
> Und so zart am Leibchen.
> Dachte dich sogleich als Braut,
> Gleich dem Reichsten angetraut,
> Dachte dich als Weibchen.[1]

This is, moreover, one of those little pictures
of maidens, which Goethe drew with a happy
hand and a sympathetic smile.   Another little
moral-satirical picture is that of the youth,
now a Baccalaureus, who introduces himself
again to Mephistopheles and again finds him,
as he found him once before, dressed in
Faust's fur robe, and resumes his former
discussion with him, but this time with a
new mind.   Here we find but one of the many
fatherly warnings which Goethe, when slightly
exasperated, gave to youths, who in his time,
too, were convinced that those who have
passed the age of thirty, the " alten Herren,"
should turn their attention to dying, since it
is with themselves, young people who have
just come to life, that the world really begins :

---

[1] " Daughter, when you came to light, I adorned you
with a little bonnet, you were so pretty to look at, your
little form was so tender.   I immediately imagined you
as a bride, I straightway betrothed you to the wealthiest
wooer, I thought of you already as a little wife. . . ."

Dies ist der Jugend edelster Beruf !
Die Welt, sie war nicht eh' ich sie erschuf ;
Die Sonne führt' ich aus dem Meer herauf ;
Mit mir begann der Mond des Wechsels Lauf.[1]

" Mr. Originality, walk off in your magnificence ! " says Mephistopheles to him, when his back is turned. " How bitterly the realization would hurt you, if you only knew that no one can think of anything clever or foolish which has not already been thought of in the past." It was such people, in truth, who annoyed Goethe intensely with their pretences, their requests, their arrogance, and many a time he lost patience with them. But after this impatient farewell, Mephistopheles immediately adds that, after all, there is little harm in it, as a few years will suffice to make such boys change their mind and that the must, however absurd it may seem when fermenting, eventually becomes wine.

The monstrous animals of ancient mythology reappear to Faust on the Pharsalian Plains. They are familiar figures to the poet who has lived so long in the world of poetry. Now he seems very glad to be able to see them near and to touch them, as it were,

---

[1] " This is the noblest career of youth ! The world did not exist before I created it ; the sun I brought up from the sea ; the moon began her course with me. . . ."

and he says with Faust, pointing to the Sphinxes :

"Before such as these Oedipus stood once " ;

and to the Sirens :

"Before such as these Ulysses crouched in hempen bands " ;

and to the Ants :

"Such were those who gathered the greatest treasure " ;

and to the Griffins :

"Such were those who guarded it faithfully and without fault."

Great forms—great memories !

Vom frischen Geiste fühl' ich mich durchdrungen,
Gestalten gross, gross die Erinnerungen.[1]

Is it an enjoyment of the imagination or a jest ? Both. The nymphs on Peneios sing him a sweet song and he again enjoys these dear images, these " dreams " or these " memories."

Ich wache ja ! O lasst sie walten
Die unvergleichlichen Gestalten
Wie sie dorthin mein Auge schickt.
So wunderbar bin ich durchdrungen !
Sind's Träume ?   Sind's Erinnerungen ?[2]

[1] " I feel imbued with fresh spirit, how great the forms, how great the memories."

[2] " I am indeed awake ! Oh let these incomparable forms, such as my eye follows thither, pursue their play. I am filled with such marvellous feelings ! Are they dreams ? Are they memories ? "

The centaur Chiron takes him on his back,
and he marvels at the personage who by
reputation was already an old acquaintance
of his :

> Der grosse Mann, der edle Pädagog,
> Der, sich zum Ruhm, ein Heldenvolk erzog,
> Den schönen Kreis der edlen Argonauten
> Und alle die des Dichters Welt erbauten.[1]

But Chiron answers with very modern com-
ments on the poor hopes of pedagogy :

> Das lassen wir an seinem Ort !
> Selbst Pallas kommt als Mentor nicht zu Ehren ;
> Am Ende treiben sie's nach ihrer Weise fort
> Als wenn sie nicht erzogen wären.[2]

Helena reappears in her resplendent beauty,
and the " scholar," or rather the well-trained
philologist, expresses some doubt, and prefers
as more reliable what is written in the texts
to what he sees with his eyes :

> Ich seh' sie deutlich, doch gesteh' ich frei,
> Zu zweifeln ist, ob sie die rechte sei.
> Die Gegenwart verführt in's Übertriebne,
> Ich halte mich vor allem an's Geschriebene.[3]

---

[1] " The great man, the noble mentor, who to his glory
brought up a race of heroes, the fine company of the Argo-
nauts and all who fashioned the poet's world."

[2] " We will pass over this ! Even Pallas as a mentor
has not won any honour ; in spite of all our teaching they
go their own way, as if they had never been educated."

[3] " I see her distinctly, but I must admit that it is
doubtful whether she is the real Helen. Seeing with one's
eyes induces one to exaggerate. I rely first and foremost
on what is written."

The little old couple, whose idyllic happiness
Faust disturbs and destroys, are adorned
and exalted with the Ovidian names of
Philemon and Baucis. With what a little
old woman's grace, attentive and affectionate,
does Baucis receive the greeting of the guest
whom she had welcomed once before, anxious
now that her husband, who is enjoying a
beneficial sleep, should not be awakened :

> Lieber Kömmling ! Leise ! Leise !
> Ruhe ! Lass den Gatten ruhn !
> Langer Schlaf verleiht dem Greise
> Kurzen Wachens rasches Thun.[1]

The scenes of the Imperial Council, with the
speeches of the Chancellor, the Treasurer,
the Marshal, the War Minister, and the other
scenes of the battle between the Emperor
and the Anti-Emperor, followed by the
conferring of rewards on those who have
contributed to the victory and by the arts
of the Archbishop who secures a large domain
for the Church, are also very graceful,
provided they are read as if they were recited
by puppets, and that one does not attempt
to find therein a political and social drama
in the manner of Shakespeare.

---

[1] " Dear stranger ! Gently ! Gently ! Hush ! Let my
husband rest ! A long sleep enables an old man to be
quick and active during his short waking."

And what witty sayings escape from the evil lips of Mephistopheles (" Krieg, Handel und Piraterie Dreieinig sind sie nicht zu trennen,"[1] etc. etc.) ; and what weighty maxims are put into the mouth of Faust from beginning to end, especially his last words, which have become famous, spoken when dying, stating what is the highest happiness on earth :

> Auf freiem Grund mit freiem Volke stehn,[2]

and the only way to deserve freedom and life :

> Nur der verdient sich Freiheit wie das Leben,
> Der täglich sie erobern muss.[3]

Amidst this wealth of sparkling cleverness and sublime wisdom rises the lyrical lament for the death of Euphorion-Byron, for whom Goethe showed such admiration, mingled with tender affection. It reminds one partly of the *Cinque Maggio* of Manzoni, an ode which Goethe translated, an elegy on the death of another great man whom he admired :

---

[1] " War, commerce and piracy are a trinity, which cannot be dissolved. . . ."
[2] " To stand on a free soil with a free people."
[3] " Only he deserves liberty and life, who must win it every day."

Doch du ranntest unaufhaltsam
Frei in's willenlose Netz,
So entzweitest du gewaltsam
Dich mit Sitte, mit Gesetz ;
Doch zuletzt das höchste Sinnen
Gab dem reinen Muth Gewicht,
Wolltest Herrliches gewinnen,
Aber es gelang dir nicht.

Wem gelingt es ?—Trübe Frage,
Der das Schicksal sich vermummt,
Wenn am unglückseligsten Tage
Blutend alles Volk verstummt.
Doch erfrischet neue Lieder,
Steht nicht länger tief gebeugt :
Denn der Boden zeugt sie wieder,
Wie von je er sie gezeugt.[1]

If we examine thus this last work of Goethe, of which we have glanced through a few pages here and there, we shall perchance enjoy it in accordance with the spirit of its author, and experience when reading it the same pleasure as the author must have experienced when composing it, free henceforth from the tumult of passion, free too

[1] " But you ran unrestrainedly and openly into the passive snare and tore yourself violently from customs and laws ; at last, however, your lofty meditation lent weight to your pure spirit, you longed to gain the most glorious prize, but you failed to do so.

Who will gain it ? Hard question, which destiny will not answer, when, on the day of bitterest sorrow, all bleeding are silent. But bring forth new songs, remain no longer with heads bowed ; for the earth will produce them again, as it has ever produced them."

from the strain of art, satisfying his caprices with his imagination and interweaving in the figures which he called up and sketched with a light hand his own thoughts and admonitions. *Faust II* is not a lamentable document of the senile decay of a genius, but a crackling of sparks when a great fire dies out, the rich close of a superlatively rich poetical and mental life.

XVI

CONCLUSION

THE hints given in the course of this short treatise can be developed and better determined by a critic who undertakes a closer study of the works of Goethe, or even by the merely intelligent reader who feels the necessity of informing himself fully about what he reads ; or this examination can be extended to some of Goethe's minor works which we either did not mention or touched on only hastily ; or certain lines can be drawn with a greater surety of touch or even in a somewhat different direction. But what I think I may affirm is that in the sphere within which I have endeavoured to remain, the criticism of Goethe (like that of any other poet and artist) must be limited and operate. Everything else, unless it is useful preparatory work, is merely academic pastime and, more often, confusion ; or it may still have some value, but no longer any value as literary criticism. We have mentioned here and there biographical notices and ideas and opinions of the poet and his time according as it was necessary for us to do so in order to illustrate the genesis of his poetry; but it should be clearly understood that if this poetry were to be examined and analysed in order to extract from it information concerning the life of the poet, his poetical, social and philosophical ideas and the spiritual changes of the time; if, in short, one were to proceed in the opposite direction (not from the man and society to poetry, but from the latter to the former), one would be leaving the sphere of literary history, and one would be leaving Goethe as a poet: so true is it that great, mediocre, and bad poets serve equally well a similar documentary purpose, and it is not at all certain that, as far as this purpose is concerned, bad poets offer less useful services than the best ones.

Nevertheless, many readers will consider that the analysis which we have carried out in this treatise is greatly defective, because we have not defined (as they say) the " position " which Goethe occupies " in the development of literary history." That may

be ; but only in the light of critical prejudice.
For in truth I know not what position Goethe
occupies in the development of literary
history, unless it is that of having been
what he was; and this is the position
which we have endeavoured to describe,
i.e. that he was just himself, Goethe, and
not this or that poet, different from himself.
Or does the reader want something else
perhaps ?

Yes, I can guess approximately what is
wanted. I can guess it, because everyone
who makes a mental analysis, sketches
certain outlines of ideas, which he discards
as unsuitable or extraneous, knowing, however, that later on he must see them rise up
before him in the form of censures, objections,
or wishes. Amongst the sketches which I
traced mentally and immediately afterwards
discarded mentally, there was a beautiful
picture of Goethe, the initiator of all the
literary forms of the nineteenth century, of
the systematized poem (*Faust*), of the auto-
biographical-sentimental novel (*Werther*), of
the novel of educational development
(*Meister*), of the historical novel and drama
(*Goetz* and *Egmont*), of the novel of passionate
and moral casuistry (the *Wahlverwandt-*

schaften), of the Utopian novel (the *Wander-jahre*), of neo-classical tragedy (*Iphigenie*), of neo-Homeric poetry (*Hermann und Dorothea*), of the revival of the ancient myths (*Achilleïs, Helena*), of the lyric in the manner of the folk-song (the *Lieder*), of ballads tragic and gnomic (the *Braut von Corinth*, the *Zauber-lehrling*), of poetry with an oriental tinge (the *Divan*), of the impassioned lyric in free verse (*Wandrers Sturmlied*, *Seefahrt*, etc.); even, one might say, of the esoterical lyric, a series of saltatory impressions connected by some deep and unexpressed ideal thread (as in the *Harzreise*); and even, if one wishes, the initiator of "free phrases," which the "Futurists" of to-day think they have invented (see any portion of the *Campagne in Frankreich*); not to mention all the separate motives which he has created and which have produced and continue to produce a large progeny, from Faust and Prometheus to Wagner and Mephistopheles, from Iphigenie, Margarete and Mignon to Marianne and Philine. This picture (to which I should not have failed to add, as an effect of contrast, that aspect of Goethe, which I have already pointed out, which entitles him to be regarded as the last great representative in the line of " Court poets," who arose in the Renaissance and who were honoured with the names of Ariosto and Tasso) I might have placed at the beginning or at the end of my treatment of the various works and as a sort of introduction to the history of poetry in the nineteenth century. I might have written in this manner very decorative and lively pages. I might have placed before my readers a brilliant historical-ideal structure, which for a moment at least would have dazzled and satisfied them, as everything does which seems to make order arise from disorder, the one from the various, the clear-cut from the confused, and all in the most simple and easy manner.

Why did I refuse to produce this effect, so pleasant for the reader, so flattering for myself ? Because this " position " assigned to Goethe, as the initiator of modern literature, as the delineator, as it were, of the programme and the prescriber of the subjects which it would execute and develop and which it would still be toiling at, may be agreeable as a play of the imagination, but does not correspond to the truth, this scrupulous truth which must be dearer to us than anything else, and after which alone we must strive, even though we may be allowed to attain it only imperfectly. Every poet is an initiator, but every poet initiates something which ends with him, because the beginning and the end are his own personality. Whoever comes after him is either a poet too, and has, therefore, a fresh personality and passes through a new and personal cycle ; or he is not a poet, and in that case may imitate and repeat what has already been discovered, but imitators, as everyone knows, do not count in the history of true poetry. Thus the initiative which Goethe is supposed to have taken in so many and such varied spheres of literature, is either to be reduced to the obvious statement that he, like every man of genius, called forth many imitators, or, at most, is to be taken in the following sense : that in Goethe's poetry, in his rich, varied, impressionable and highly intelligent mind were mirrored for the first time in conspicuous fashion many sides of the modern spirit, which, helped certainly by his example, were afterwards mirrored in other poets and artists too. This second statement is true also, but forms precisely the subject of extraneous consideration and belongs to the history of culture, since in the history of poetry what is of primary importance is the particular manner of these reflections, the individual minds of the poets and the perfection of form attained by diverse and individual methods. It is hardly necessary to add that by attributing to Goethe the fantastic function of literary initiator in general of modern times, thus giving free passage to the work of imagination, one is induced to proceed from exaggeration to exaggeration ; and, in order to form a fine idol, one easily forgets the " motives in modern literature " of which one finds no examples in Goethe's works, and one passes in silence over those which he took from predecessors and contemporaries, who were not always Germans.

Therefore I have refused an easy, but not a legitimate enrichment of these brief notes, and I have left them in their poverty, in that poverty which, as everyone knows, is often sister to honesty.

INDEX

205